MW00770450

EDGAR CAYCE ON
VIBRATIONS

Selected Books by Kevin J. Todeschi

EDGAR CAYCE ON
VIBRATIONS
Spirit in Motion

By
Kevin J. Todeschi

A.R.E. Press • Virginia Beach • Virginia

A.R.E. Press
215 67th Street
Virginia Beach, VA 23451-2061

Library of Congress Cataloging-in-Publication Data
Todeschi, Kevin J.
    Edgar Cayce on vibrations : spirit in motion / by Kevin J. Todeschi.
        p. cm.
    Includes bibliographical references.
    ISBN 13: 978-0-87604-567-1 (trade pbk.)
    1. Cayce, Edgar, 1877-1945. 2. Vibration–Miscellanea. I. Title.
    BF1999.T57 2007
    133.8092–dc22

                                                            2007014013

Cover design by Richard Boyle

Table of Contents

Life in its manifestation is vibration.

—Edgar Cayce

PREFACE

EVERYTHING IS VIBRATION. EVERYTHING IS IN MOTION. In spite of how the physical world may appear to the naked eye, science has proven that all of materiality—consisting of atoms and therefore protons, neutrons, and electrons—is in motion.

Most of us can probably understand how vibrations might be compared to the ripples that occur when a stone is dropped in a pool of water. The truth, however, is that vibrations are much, much more. Light, for example, is a vibration. The eye is essentially a mechanical device that transforms light waves into electrical impulses which travel to the brain, where they are translated into "images" that give the perception of sight. Similarly, sound is a vibration. The ear, too, is a mechanical device that transforms the vibration of sound into electrical impulses. These impulses further travel through the nerves into the brain. Likewise, the senses of taste and smell entail extracting vibrations and ultimately transforming those vibrations into impulses that are deciphered by the brain. Information from the senses is relayed or transported as energy from one point to another in the form of waves.

Twentieth-century experiments in physics gave rise to the wave-particle duality, which is simply that light waves of energy in some experiments behave like particles, and particles of matter in some experiments behave like waves of energy. Therefore, quantum theory contends that all matter is in motion because particles of matter fundamentally behave as a wave, and waves are essentially vibrations that repeat continuously. Everything is vibration.

The importance that vibration plays in our lives cannot be underestimated. According to R.E.D. Bishop, a distinguished professor of mechanical engineering and fellow of the University College London, vibration is all about us:

> **After all, our hearts beat, our lungs oscillate, we shiver when we are cold, we sometimes snore, we can hear and speak because our eardrums and our larynges vibrate. The light waves which permit us to see entail vibration. We move by oscillating our legs. We cannot even say "vibration" properly without the tip of the tongue oscillating. And the matter does not end there–far from it. Even the atoms of which we are constituted vibrate. It is not exaggeration to say that it is unlikely that there is any branch of science in which this phenomenon does not play an important role.**
> **Bishop, pg. 1**

It was the Greeks who first theorized the concept of atoms as the building blocks of all matter, believing that different forms of matter were made up of different types and shapes of atoms. The word *atom* comes from the Greek word *atomos*, which means "indivisible." The Greek philosopher Democritus (ca. fifth century BC) contended that if any form of matter were repeatedly subdivided, eventually a point would be reached whereby that matter could no longer be divided—that point would be an atom. His theory of atomism hypothesized that nothing existed but these different kinds, shapes, and sizes of atoms and the void in which they moved (Jewish Encyclopedia, pg. 274). These atoms moved because of their vibrations and velocities, impacting with other atoms and creating and destroying various forms of matter in the process.

Later, the Greek philosopher Plato (ca. 427-347 BC) theorized that humanity's perception of the world was essentially a shadow of true reality. In Book VII of *The Republic*, Plato describes a world in which men are imprisoned by chains attached to their legs and necks—unable to move or to see anything but the movement of shadows cast on the wall of the cave before their eyes. In this world of chains the prisoners only see the reflections cast by the shadows of reality behind them. This concept of only being able to see a shadow of true reality is relevant to the topic of vibrations in that our senses provide us with a perception of the material world that is essentially a shadow of the truth. We think we perceive reality, when in reality, we perceive the effects of the vibrations we encounter rather than being able to perceive those vibrations directly.

In spite of our inability to perceive vibrations firsthand, the concept of vibrations has nonetheless become a part of mainstream culture. For example, the 1960s pop song "Good Vibrations" by Brian Wilson of the Beach Boys describes how people put off vibrations through their emotions. That concept has further expanded so that today the idea that certain people possess "good vibes" while others put off "bad vibes" has become a part of everyday language.

The possibility that individuals could actually put off good vibes or bad vibes and have an effect on the material world moved beyond anecdotal accounts and stories into the realm of science with the publication of Masaru Emoto's international bestseller *The Messages of Water* in 1999. Emoto's work demonstrated that the vibration of the environment or the vibration of an individual in the environment has an influence upon the molecular shape of water crystals. Although some might not be surprised to learn that this vibration can come from music and spoken words, Emoto found evidence that water was also influenced by the vibrations of thought, the written word, and even pictures and images. Everything has a vibration and that vibration has been shown to have an effect upon the formation of water crystals. His research has recorded the effect of various types of music upon water crystals, the spoken word in a variety of languages, even the vibrations of thoughts and the written word, which he describes here:

We next thought about what would happen if we wrote words or phrases like "Thank you" and "Fool" on pieces of paper, and wrapped the paper around the bottles of water with the words facing in. It didn't seem logical for water to "read" the writing, understand the meaning, and change its form accordingly. But . . . the results of the experiments didn't disappoint us. Water exposed to "Thank you" formed beautiful hexagonal crystals, but water exposed to the word "Fool" produced crystals similar to the water exposed to heavy-metal music, malformed and fragmented.

Further experimenting showed that water exposed to positive expressions like "Let's do it!" created attractive, well-formed crystals, but the water exposed to negative expressions like "Do it!" barely formed any crystals at all.

The lesson that we can learn from this experiment has to do with the power of words. The vibration of good words has a positive effect on our world, whereas the vibration from negative words has the power to destroy.

Emoto, pgs. xxiv-xxv

The implications of his findings are especially far-reaching when one considers that the human body is approximately 70 percent water. With this in mind, every word, image, and thought that individuals encounter in life, including the thoughts of others, cannot help but have a positive or a negative vibrational impact upon their physical bodies.

Interestingly enough, Emoto's work also inadvertently confirmed one of the premises from a unique source—the psychic work of Edgar Cayce. Called the "father of holistic medicine" and "the most documented psychic of all time," Edgar Cayce (1877–1945) became known for his incredible accuracy and for a psychic legacy that continues to help and inspire individuals all over the world. (Additional biographical information can be found in *There Is a River* by Thomas Sugrue and *Edgar Cayce an American Prophet* by Sidney Kirkpatrick.) Cayce contended that every thought essentially possesses an energetic vibration leading to the creation of "crimes or miracles" because of the impact of that vibration—literally healing or harming at some level everyone to whom the thought is directed. For example, during the course of a reading given to a forty-four-year-old businessman, Cayce admonished him to become aware of what was motivating his thoughts as well as his ultimate goal in his relationships with others. The reading asked, "Are thy thoughts always prompted by the desire to be of help to others? or are they the more often prompted by the desire to use *others* as thy stepping-stones to better things for thyself?" Along the same lines, the reading counseled him, "Know that thoughts are things, and as their currents run they may become crimes or miracles." (2419-1[1])

In spite of the hundreds of books written about the Edgar Cayce material, relatively little exploration has been done on the wealth of information Cayce provided dealing with the topic of vibration. Even students of the Cayce legacy may be surprised to learn that the subject is discussed in more than twenty-five hundred readings. These readings suggest that all force is vibratory in nature, and they explore the topic of vibrations in terms of consciousness, healing, the material world, even the nature of God and physical reality. One of the few individuals to thoroughly examine the Cayce material on vibrations was longtime Cayce scholar Everett Irion, who stated:

> **Vibration is not only a deep subject, with far-reaching implications; it is a vast one, encompassing mathematical areas such as geometry and optics, the aesthetics of color, such metaphysical considerations as the nature of time and space, and various philosophical and theological concepts.**
> **Irion, pgs. vii-viii**

Irion pointed out that even though vibrations are the basis for all matter (and even consciousness) that exists, the subject remained relatively unknown by most individuals in spite of its importance. On one occasion, he used an analogy comparing vibrations to the roots of a tree in a forest. Although the roots support and feed the tree and without the roots the tree would not exist—no one ever cares about the

---

[1] The Edgar Cayce readings are numbered to maintain confidentiality. The first set of numbers (for example, "2419") refers to the individual or group for whom the reading was given. The second set of numbers (for example, "1") refers to the number of the reading for that individual or group.

roots. However, just as without the roots the tree could not exist, without vibration, there isn't anything at all that could exist.

Another Cayce scholar and researcher, David McMillin, has found an amazing similarity between the Cayce information on vibrations and the nature of physical reality as it is theorized by the Superstring theory of physics. The Superstring theory essentially describes how the primary forces of nature are all just different manifestations of the same one force—this is the same underlying premise of vibrations and the oneness of all force that is found in the Cayce readings. McMillin points this out:

> ... string theory is based on the premise of extremely small vibrating strings that are the basis for all manifestations of energy and matter. Theoretically, the frequency and resonance at which the strings vibrate result in all the variations of matter that we find all about us ranging from apples and oranges to vast swirling galaxies. It's all the same stuff vibrating at different rates–a virtual music of the spheres.
>
> That is exactly the way Edgar Cayce described the nature of physical reality. At a practical level, Cayce explained health and illness within the human body as a matter of vibratory rates. Each organ of the body vibrates at its own specific frequency. Too much or too little energy can result in vibratory imbalances. Various vibrational energy medicine therapies prescribed in the readings are intended to work with the vibratory energies of the body.
>
> String theory provides a conceptual model for understanding how vibration is the basis for understanding how the human body and the universe in its totality are created and maintained. It is easy to see why enthusiasts for this approach call it a "theory of everything."
>
> McMillin, *Venture Inward*

The Cayce readings confirm much that science has proved or theorized about the nature of vibration. In terms of each of the physical senses operating through the use of vibrations, in 1932 Cayce had this to say:

. . . as we find in the physical body that sight, hearing, taste, speech, are but an alteration of vibration attuned to those portions in the consciousness of the physical body, becoming aware *of* things, *of* vibration, reaching same from within or from without . . .   281-4

The readings contend that all of creation emanates from one source—*spirit*—and that one force continues to be integrally connected to the material world and lies at the basis of its movement and vibration:

For, returning to the first principle–as there are those forces that move one within another to bring harmony, as for light or color, or sound, or motion, all of these are but the variation of movement, vibration. What is the First Cause? That from which all emanates, the *spirit* of the force or influence itself; breaking itself upon the atomic structures about same, bringing those influences as it associates itself one with another in its varied forms of atomic structure.
                                                              2012-1

And:

The basis, then: "Know, O Israel, (Know, O People) the Lord Thy God is One!"
From this premise we would reason, that: In the manifestation of all power, force, motion, vibration, that which impels, that which detracts, is in its essence of one force, one source, in its elemental form.   262-52

In terms of vibration and human emotions and activity, the work of Masaru Emoto suggests that each human being creates a vibration that is unique to that individual. According to Emoto's findings:

Human beings are also vibrating, and each individual vibrates at a unique frequency. Each one of us has the sensory skills necessary to feel the vibrations of others.

> A person experiencing great sadness will emit a sadness
> frequency, and someone who is always joyful and living life
> fully will emit a corresponding frequency. A person who loves
> others will send out a frequency of love, but from a person
> who acts out evil will come a dark and evil frequency.
>
> Emoto, pg. 41

Along these same lines, the Edgar Cayce readings assert that an individual's level of consciousness creates a vibration all its own. People also affect one another (both consciously and unconsciously, and positively and negatively) with their personal vibration. On the negative end of the spectrum, someone that is generally angry, depressed, negative, or somehow unbalanced might be described as possessing bad vibes or somehow "draining" to be around. On the positive end of the spectrum, someone who is most often optimistic, inspirational, or genuinely spiritual can come across as an individual who, by her or his very presence, is motivational, nurturing, compassionate, or even a healing presence. In fact, the possibility of possessing such a heightened vibration that it can somehow positively impact and raise the vibrations in another person, facilitating healing in the process, is described in Scripture on numerous occasions.

One such story clearly illustrating the possibility of an individual being healed simply by coming in contact with a being possessing a higher level of consciousness is described in the biblical account of the woman being healed of uninterrupted (menstrual?) bleeding. According to Scripture, she was healed simply because of coming in contact with Jesus and His vibration:

> And a woman having an issue of blood twelve years, which
> had spent all her living upon physicians, neither could be
> healed of any,
> Came behind him, and touched the border of his gar-
> ment: and immediately her issue of blood stanched.
> And Jesus said, Who touched me? When all denied,
> Peter and they that were with him said, Master, the
> multitude throng thee and press thee, and sayest thou, Who
> touched me?

And Jesus said, Somebody hath touched me: for I perceive that is gone out of me. Luke 8:43-46

In terms of healing and the physical body, the Cayce material suggests that each organ within the physical body possesses an optimum vibration. Furthermore, the readings contend that illness and "dis–ease" often manifest when that physical organ is no longer attuned to that optimum vibration. With this in mind, healing is best facilitated through a variety of measures, all designed to assist the body and its organisms in returning to the proper vibration. Those measures might include a variety of treatments, such as medicine, surgery, physical adjustments, changes in lifestyle or attitude, and even energy work. Regardless of the treatment, however, the goal is primarily to help facilitate the body itself in a return to wholeness and even an awareness of its connection to the one force. In the language of the readings:

For, all healing comes from the one source. And whether there is the application of foods, exercise, medicine, or even the knife–it is to bring the consciousness of the forces within the body that aid in reproducing themselves–the awareness of creative or God forces. 2696-1

Confirming the premise behind Plato's story of the prisoners bound in the cave, the readings admonish that we are indeed seeing shadows of reality rather than the reality behind those shadows: ". . . all one sees manifest in a material world is but a reflection or a shadow of the real or the spiritual life." (262–23) Essentially, the shadows we see are simply our perceptions of the material world; the truth behind those shadows, however, has its origins in the spiritual dimension. The spirit is absolutely essential in any discussion of vibrations because, from Cayce's perspective, the one force that is currently theorized by the Superstring theory would best be described as the Creative, or God, force. Examples of this premise permeate the readings and include the following:

All force is vibration, as all comes from one central vibration

and its activity into, out from, and its own creative forces, as given, with that of the divine as manifested in man, is same vibration–taking different form. 900-422

. . . for matter is an expression of spirit in motion . . . 262-78

Electricity or vibration is that same energy, same power, ye call God. Not that God is an electric light or an electric machine, but that vibration that is creative is of that same energy as life itself. 2828-4

As is understood, Life–God–in its essence is Vibration . . . 281-4

The all–pervading presence of vibration has its foundation in the one force of the divine spirit, and all vibration is ultimately that spirit in motion and the variety of ways in which spirit has manifested in the material world. That one force and the vibrations associated with all aspects of the material world continue to affect each and every one of us. With that in mind, this book was written with the hope that it might make a contribution to our collective understanding of the nature of vibrations, how we continue to create and shape those vibrations, how vibrations impact the world around us, how all of life is vibration, and how vibrations are ultimately spirit in motion.

VIBRATIONS
Edgar Cayce on Vibration

For, all vibrations are part of the universal consciousness with each and every entity.   1921-1

THE FIRST MENTION OF THE TERM *vibration* in the Edgar Cayce material appears to have occurred on July 26, 1909, when Edgar Cayce was asked to give a reading by a father who was concerned about the health of his son. The child was twenty-one-months old and was suffering from dizzy spells and an infection in the knee that was creating problems with the boy's right leg, causing the child to be weak and hesitant to take more than a few steps. The boy also had a difficult time sitting up straight. In spite of the fact that the boy's parents had sought conventional medical help, the doctors had been unable to treat the child's condition.

More than forty years later, the boy's sister supplied the Edgar Cayce archives with her memory of her brother's situation:

> The doctors thought there was an infection in the knee joint,
> for he cried whenever he put any weight on his right leg and
> finally could not walk at all . . . it was becoming painful for
> him to sit up. His knee was badly swollen and inflamed and
> the doctors were planning to put his leg in a cast.
>
> 4468-1 Reports

Complicating the family's situation at the time of the reading was the
fact that the father was in Indiana on an extended business trip, while
the mother, the son, and the couple's other children were in Little Rock,
Arkansas. When the boy's father heard from his wife that their son's
condition had worsened, he immediately wrote to Edgar Cayce for a
reading. In spite of the fact that Edgar Cayce was in Alabama at the time
of the reading and the boy was in Arkansas, Cayce was somehow
psychically able to provide a thorough description of the problem as
well as a suggested course of treatment. More than one year later, the
father would sign a sworn affidavit for a Boston research society,
testifying to the efficacy of Cayce's work. This is the content of that
affidavit:

> November 21, 1910
> The following is my testimony regarding the illness of my
> child and the invaluable service Mr. Edgar Cayce rendered in
> affecting his cure.
> On or about July 17th, 1909, our baby boy 21 months old
> was taken very sick with a high fever, temperature 103, for
> 24 hours a physician was summoned and baby continued
> worse beginning to jerk considerably, which continued
> several days. Even after fever subsided, and was unable to
> hold himself up. Previous to being sick he was a very stout
> and healthy child walking and running everywhere. Two
> weeks went by and he was still unable to sit or stand,
> although without fever. Appetite good, but when he would
> attempt to stand he would fall and cry. Physician attending
> him all the time. After the fever subsided the doctor assured
> me the worse was over, so I continued my work on the road.
> It was after my leaving home that they discovered that
> baby's inability to walk. My wife became alarmed and wrote

me the situation. I wrote Mr. Edgar Cayce at Bowling Green, Ky. [Cayce would be in Alabama at the time of the reading] and asked him to diagnose the case, giving him Mrs. Putman's address in Little Rock Ark. He immediately sent her a diagnosis and a copy of same to me at Terre Haute, Ind.

At the time the above occurred my wife was visiting in Little Rock and on receiving Mr. Cayce's diagnosis returned to Bowling Green, Ky. and placed baby under the care of Dr. T. W. Posey, osteopath. After reading diagnosis given by Mr. Cayce, Dr. Posey pronounced it true to his own. He treated the child nearly two months and dismissed him as cured. He is now three years old and in seeming perfect health. I take worlds of pleasure in making this sworn statement in behalf of Mr. Cayce, as it is very likely that our little boy would not be with us today in a bright, happy, healthy condition, both mentally and physically, had it not been through his assistance. I hope that his testimonial will aid some one else to find as much joy through his assistance as we have.

Respectfully, F. O. Putnam, 1600 Park Ave., Little Rock, Ark.
Subscribed and sworn to before me this 21st day of Nov. 1910
[signed] E. R. Ratterres–Notary Public

The reading stated that the child's condition had caused a breakdown of the functioning of his internal organs. As a result, he was experiencing nausea, an enlarged liver, an excess of bile, immobility, an overtaxing of the kidneys, and a problem with circulation. The bowels were also impacted with excess waste material, which was aggravating the situation. If left untreated, Cayce warned that the condition might lead to paralysis as well as a curvature of the spine. The suggested treatments included a stimulation of the child's nervous system, especially through the use of "vibrations" resulting from osteopathic adjustments and manipulation and a stimulation of the child's elimination processes. The reading would be the first time that the Cayce information tied vibrations into the subject of health and healing, but it would certainly not be the last. Between 1909 and 1944 more than one thousand readings would discuss the importance of vibrations in connection with health, healing, and the treatment of illness and disease.

From Cayce's perspective, each organ and function of the body is designed to operate in an optimal manner. That optimal manner creates a resonance, or a vibration, that maintains equilibrium, enabling the organ to function properly and work in connection with every other system in the body. When a physical function or one of the body's organs is not working properly, there is a resultant discordant vibration that impacts the entire physical body. The readings suggest that not only does each system have its proper vibration but also that vibration can be used through various means in conjunction with other healing modalities to facilitate healing. Therefore, one aspect of Cayce's approach to healing is to create the means whereby the body's systems can return to their optimum vibration, and the body becomes a cooperative partner in the healing process.

As will be discussed later, health readings were given for every imaginable problem and disease afflicting individuals in the first half of the twentieth century. Depending upon the illness, Cayce recommended treatments including everything from surgery and medicine to exercise, a change in diet, osteopathic and chiropractic adjustments, physiotherapy, and a change of attitude. In fact, Cayce's "medicine chest" frequently drew upon a variety of healthcare practitioners. Therefore, it is a mistake to assume that the readings only focused on homeopathic and naturopathic remedies, as depending on the condition, they also recommended various allopathic, pharmacological, and surgical approaches.

One example of a health reading from the Cayce files that has a great deal to do with the subject of vibrations concerns a middle-aged woman who made this request for help: "I have been in bad health for several years and having heard of some of your work am in great hope that you can tell me a cure for my trouble." Although she was only thirty-seven-years old, the woman's complaints included nausea, vertigo, a tingling, or "needle pricks," in the extremities of her body, nerve strain, depression, cold feet, hot flashes, stiffness in the joints, and indigestion.

During the course of the reading, Cayce systematically examined and commented upon the functioning of each of the body's major systems and organs, including the blood circulation and supply, the nervous system, brain, throat, heart, lungs, stomach, digestion, liver, pancreas, kidneys, elimination processes, and so forth. Overall, the reading suggested that the main cause of the woman's multiple problems was toxemia—somehow toxins had accumulated within the physical body and these toxins were now being circulated throughout the bloodstream. The problem had essentially occurred because of improper diet, poor eliminations, nervous strain, improper digestion, and the resultant strain on various organs. Demonstrating how each of the body's systems was interconnected as well as describing the interrelationship between vibrations and physical health, Cayce's statements to the woman included the following:

> . . . for, as we find, the body–*each* body–made up of vibratory force and of cellular conditions within the physical forces, that are as small worlds or universes within themselves, and the blood stream that which correlates the ability of each of these atomic forces to work in unison throughout the system.
>
> This not a deficiency, but a lack of coordination between the nerve systems–which are as a unit, yet function one with each within itself–for remember, each organism, and each vibratory force as set in the body, is as of a unit within itself– and they are of the countless millions! See?
>
> Now, to meet the needs of these conditions in this body, it becomes necessary, as we see, then, to create the correct vibration, and remove from the body these conditions in the normal way, without disturbing the equilibrium of the functioning of any organ above or below in its (the organ's) normal condition . . . we would create that *correct* vibration that will bring about the normal forces to each portion, and especially stimulating the blood supply to that condition wherein *it* (the blood supply) may be kept nearer normal throughout, and at all times.   121-1

Cayce's course of treatment included a change of diet, improved eliminations, several therapies designed to help improve the woman's digestive and assimilation processes, and a stimulation of the circulation through such things as massage. The reading also prescribed the use of a Cayce-recommended electrical appliance (which will be discussed in later chapters), designed to stimulate and assist the body in its return to proper functioning. By following the recommended course of treatment, the reading assured the woman that the condition could be "eliminated through the proper channels" and would result in the creation of "that proper vibration within the body."

In addition to vibrations and health, the Cayce material provides a wealth of information on the topic of vibrations and consciousness. Essentially, this material suggests that as individuals raise their own consciousness and attune to higher levels of spirit and vibration, they can become channels for the one force and become co-creative partners with the divine in bringing spirit into the earth. Beginning in 1931, two types of group readings started taking place that explored this premise in greater detail. One was the study group readings, which were given to a group of individuals that called themselves Norfolk #1, and the other was the prayer group readings, which were given to the Glad Helpers Prayer Group. Both of these sets of materials continue to have a major impact upon the Cayce work even to this day, and both ultimately provide a series of tools for transforming personal consciousness and raising individual vibration.

As background information, it is important to point out one of the major premises contained in what might be called the Cayce cosmology. From the perspective of the Cayce readings, rather than being physical bodies that possess souls, each individual is ultimately a spiritual being, a soul, having a physical experience. Through life's experiences and individual soul growth, each soul will ultimately reawaken to its divine source and acquire an awareness of its oneness with the rest of creation. The readings contend that this reawakening occurred in the life of Jesus and is perhaps best described as the universal Christ Consciousness: "the awareness within each soul, imprinted in pattern on the mind and waiting to be awakened by the will, of the soul's oneness with God." (5749-14) Rather than being connected to a particular religion, Cayce called Jesus the "elder brother" for all of humanity and stated that this Christ Consciousness is universal and is the destiny for every soul regardless of his or her religious beliefs. In fact, Cayce suggests that God desired to bring spirit into the earth and that each individual is destined to become an emissary of that spirit, ultimately raising the vibration of the earth and the third dimension to be in accord with divine will.

For example, in 1932, while giving a discourse on the subject of prayer, meditation, and vibration, Cayce told the Glad Helpers Prayer Group that as they raised their personal vibration through attunement and spiritual growth, they would experience a "closer walk" with God. This would also enable them to become channels of spiritual energy to others. In the language of the readings, the group was reminded that:

> **Vibration is, in its simple essence or word, *raising* the Christ Consciousness in self to such an extent as it may flow *out* of self to him thou would direct it to . . . What produces same? These are the *vibrations* to which a body has raised by its attunement of its whole being, its whole inner self, of a consciousness of that divine force that emanates in Life itself in this material plane.** 281-7

Echoing this same premise, on another occasion, a forty-five-year-old woman seeking mental and spiritual counsel from Edgar Cayce was encouraged with advice as to the ultimate purpose for which each soul enters into the earth:

> **The purpose of the entity in the earth, is that it may know itself, also to be itself, and yet at one with the Creative Forces, fulfilling those purposes for which the entity comes into the earth; accepting, believing, knowing then thy relationship to that Creative Force.** 3508-1

Throughout a series of readings given to the Norfolk #1 Study Group, Edgar Cayce described how the application of spiritual principles in the earth led to a growth in consciousness as well as a higher personal vibration. However, even group members might have been surprised in 1934 when a reading described how every location also possesses its own unique vibration, essentially created by the people and activities within the surrounding area. Cayce told those assembled: "This might be interesting to those who are compiling things. Each state, country, or town makes its own vibrations by or through the activities of those that comprise same . . ." (262-66) In other words, the collective thoughts and activities of a group of people in a location create an energetic vibration that is reflective of those very thoughts and activities. As unusual as this may sound to some, the feeling inside a church, synagogue, or mosque—even if you are the only individual present—is very different from the feeling inside a very different place, such as a post office, even if you are the only individual present. Somehow collective thought and activity help to energize a place with vibration. With this in mind, is it any wonder, then, that individuals sometimes feel out of sync with a particular location?—suggesting perhaps that the individual's energetic vibration is somehow out of harmony with (or very different from) the collective whole.

In addition to vibrations being integrally connected to healing, consciousness, and locations, everything that is a part of the material world is also subject to vibrations and ultimately emanates vibrations all its own. On one occasion, Cayce told a thirty-four-year-old physicist:

> **For . . . everything in motion, everything that has taken on materiality as to become expressive in any kingdom in the material world, is *by* the *vibrations* that are the motions—or those positive and negative influences that make for that differentiation that man has called matter in its various stages of evolution into material things.** **699-1**

Interestingly enough, the same individual was encouraged to use his first initial and his middle name, "J. Howard," rather than his first name (John), as it apparently created a vibration more in keeping with the talents and abilities he was attempting to manifest in his life at that time. Therefore, names and words possess individual vibrations as well.

On one occasion, an individual who was very interested in the vibrational qualities of astronomy, numbers, metals, and stones obtained a reading and inquired as to how the vibrations of each might best be used to help him in his life. Much like the information on vibrations and consciousness, Cayce suggested that ultimately, each could best be used as a means of attuning to the divine. The individual's advice included the following:

As these are but lights, but signs in thine experience, they are as but a candle that one stumbles not in the dark. But worship *not* the light of the candle; rather that to which it may guide thee in thy service. So, whether from the vibrations of numbers, of metals, of stones, these are merely to become the necessary influences to make thee in attune, one with the Creative Forces; just as the pitch of a song of praise is not the song nor the message therein, but is a helpmeet for those that would find strength in the service of the Lord. So, use them to attune self. How, ye ask? As ye apply, ye are given the next step.   707-2

Other readings discussed the connection of vibrations with music, gems, colors, and so forth. Again, everything that is a part of the material world possesses a unique vibration.

More than simply discussing metaphysical and theoretical concepts related to vibrations, the readings also confirm the findings of science in describing how vibrations are used by the nervous system to relay information from the body's sensory system to the brain. Each of the senses operates at a different vibration, and from Cayce's perspective, the capacity of speech is the highest vibration among the five senses:

Each functioning organ of the sensory system reflects a different vibration to produce to the brain the functioning of that organ, that is the sense of taste, which is based both through the tongue and at the root of the tongue and is connected with the sensory organs and to the pneumogastric nerve, and to the brain three million times less than the vibration necessary to produce hearing or sight, that of speech being even three times greater than the sense of hearing or sight; that is the highest vibration we have in the body at all.   5681-1

In addition to the above topics and their interaction with vibrations, approximately two thousand readings recommended the use of one of several Cayce-prescribed appliances to facilitate healing, most frequently either a "radio-active" appliance or a wet cell appliance. Both will be discussed in greater detail, but essentially, each uses a gentle electrical current and vibration to help normalize, equalize, or even stimulate the body's own vibratory rate, facilitating the body's ability to heal and regenerate itself.

Taken together, the Cayce information on vibrations suggests that every particular of matter, every thought, and every impulse of the spirit is indeed connected to vibrations. Everything is vibration. With this in mind, the more we can come to understand the nature of vibrations and how they operate in the world in which we live, the more we will move beyond simply perceiving the shadows of reality— the visual effects of the vibrations around us. Instead, an exploration of vibrations can enable us to come to understand the nature of ourselves, the universe in which we live and, ultimately, even our connection to the divine.

VIBRATIONS
Vibrations and Healing

Now, to give the relief necessary to bring the body to its normal forces . . . we find each system in the system, that is, the spiritual and soul forces and the physical force in all bodies produce an individual vibration, but they must co-ordinate to keep balance in the physical force. See?

3847-1

THE READINGS CONTEND THAT virtually any health problem, illness, or disease has a negative impact upon the normal functioning of the body, and that negative impact also includes an alteration of the "perfect vibration or equalization" normally associated with the affected organ or system. With this in mind, a thirty–six–year–old teacher was informed: "Every individual entity is on certain vibrations. Every dis–ease or disease is creating in the body the opposite or non-coordinant vibration with the conditions in a body–mind and spirit of the individual." (1861-12)

Since each organ and system has its corresponding healthy vibration, the Cayce approach to healing often included healing modalities designed to rebalance the body's own vibratory energies. These methods were designed to help the body become a cooperative participant in the healing process. For example, an individual who had an intestinal infection was given a series of suggested treatments in order to overcome the condition, while being told: "We would take that into the system that will give the correct vibrations to those parts affected, see, and they will give the force and vibration necessary to produce the incentives of the warrior forces in the system to overcome the condition . . ." (1323-1)

Similarly, a child diagnosed with asthenia—a debilitating physical condition that is characterized by a lack of bodily strength—was given a series of recommended therapies and counseled that one of the medicinal formulas was specifically designed "to give the correct balance in the system and to produce the correct vibration necessary to overcome this condition . . ." (4303-1)

A woman with anemia, dermatitis, heart palpitations, headaches, and spinal and assimilation problems was informed that the origination of much of her trouble was traceable to her spinal problems and a strain on the nerves in that area. Her reading stated: "These hinder the body from giving the correct vibrations to the organs there, so that correct elimination and assimilation are not made at all times, hence the body uses often times its reserve energy and vitality." (4642-1) The list of recommendations to correct her condition included spinal adjustments, increased circulation, activities in the open air and breathing exercises, as well as a diet consisting of foods with a more healthful vibration: ". . . no meats but of vegetable forces as carry much of nerve and purifying forces in their vibration, see, so assimilation and elimination be given through their proper channels, so vibration to the body will be of the correct forces to give the stimulation to blood to rebuild properly, and to produce the elimination with plenty of oxygen and air to this system."

In human physiology, there is a term called *homeostasis*, which is essentially the ability of a balanced, normal body to maintain an internal, coordinated stability of each of the body organs and systems.

This goal to assist each individual in achieving homeostasis is definitely a component of the Cayce information on health, healing, and vibration. For example, it is essentially this same process that the readings refer to when Cayce gave a reading to a forty-seven–year–old man and discussed how a healthy, normal body had the capacity to help heal itself. The reading was given in August 1929:

> **Here may well be given the condition as takes place, as to how a body organically–when the body has reached its normal development, resuscitates or rebuilds itself. It has long been confirmed that the body in toto renews itself in ever so many periods, or so many cycles of change. It is seen that not all portions of the system move in the same cycle, for the vibration that is necessary to create that tissue which will replenish a heart cell, or a ventricle, will not move in the same cycle as one that replenishes the glands of digestion, whether it be the salivary glands themselves or those of the lactice, or lacteal glands, or mammary glands, or the adrenal gland, or the thyroid gland, or those of the ducts as in the gall duct, or the pancreas, or that of the spleen in itself.**
>
> **108-2**

The concept was also described to another individual:

> **For, each portion of the body vibrates at a certain rate; or there are the electrical reactions, as life or vibration is the life of each organ. Each organ must have within itself that relative relation to the body-forces as to enable it to reproduce itself. Hence it has its particular rate of activity.**
>
> **337-27**

On another occasion, a woman was told that the root cause of her problem was that there had not been that coordinated response within her body, enabling each of the organs within her system to operate at its optimum vibration. Instead, once one of the systems of her body had gotten out of balance, various problems had occurred as the body tried to maintain its equilibrium:

. . . for as we see, each organism has its own vibration to produce that necessary for each of the forces in the building up of the organ itself, that atomic force in each cell, see? the lack of coordination brings about the distress to the nervous system, especially the sympathetic, see? All centers, then, become involved, and there is produced the headaches, the nausea, the tiredness in extremities, the swelling in portions of the body–this all, the system attempting to create an equilibrium.   139-3

As stated previously, the readings' premise is that every system and organ of the body carries a vibration that must be in balance for the body to function normally and maintain health, healing, and wellness. On one occasion, a twenty–four–year–old man complaining of eye problems, speech problems, and nerve strain was given information on the importance of proper vibrations and health. He was told that vibrations that were not in balance affected the functioning of organs within the body. Bringing those vibrations to normal functioning would help the body heal itself. He was informed: "All . . . cellular forces in the physical body have units of life of electrical or nerve force, all life being electrical in that it is vibratory. With an excess of vibrations, either organs become affected or functioning of same." (5453-1) Interestingly enough, the same individual was informed that his problems with speech were also connected to his eye problems. Cayce suggested that an improper vibration in one organ or sense could affect nearby organs to also become out of balance. By following the recommended treatments, the individual was assured that healing would come to every organ that had been affected.

From the readings' perspective, virtually any health condition affects the normal vibration and functioning. Measures that were frequently recommended to help the body return to health and proper vibration often included the following: improved eliminations, exercise (especially gentle stretching exercises), massage, diet, chiropractic or osteopathic manipulation, and more. Even when surgery, medicine, and other allopathic treatments were utilized in a patient's care, Edgar Cayce often commented on the fact that these measures either carried a helpful vibration themselves or would somehow positively influence the vibrations of the affected area. For example, on one occasion, hormone injections were recommend for a woman who had been unable to conceive and was diagnosed with sterility. Cayce stated that those injections would help stimulate the proper vibration within her body so that within four to six months, that vibration would create the necessary conditions for conception to take place. (3980-1)

A forty-seven-year-old male who had received surgery in order to remove a large, rectal polyp, described as being the size of a "small pear," obtained a follow-up reading to discern his prognosis for a complete recovery. Since the surgery occurred in 1940, a large incision had been made through the abdominal wall, and it was not healing properly. The man's secretary was worried about him and wrote Mr. Cayce her own thoughts as a cover letter to her boss's request for assistance. She described her concerns:

> **I saw him yesterday and he has a hole in the middle of his abdomen that you could stick your whole fist into. And, I would feel much better if a few more days were past and I could feel sure that [he] is out of the woods. Frankly, although everyone is very optimistic I am very much worried about him, although I have not said that to him. So far, they have sewed him up four times and the stitches have not held. It seems to me there must be something more wrong there than the doctors are telling and I know you can find out what is really wrong and tell them how to correct it. And, you are the only one who can do this for him.**
>
> **257-222 Background**

When the reading was given, Cayce stated that the internal healing was occurring much more rapidly than the external area of the incision appeared to be healing. The reading suggested that the medicines and antiseptic prescribed by the physician were helpful and should be continued. Part of the man's problem was traceable to the anesthesia slowing down the proper functioning of the nervous system; however, according to the reading, the essential cause was that the normal functioning of vibrations had been disturbed, making it impossible for the incision to heal properly. When asked why the wound had not healed and had begun to seep even eight days after the operation, Cayce replied, "The lack of the vibrations being such as to cause the coagulations." In terms of whether or not the problem would be eliminated, the response came, "This may be entirely eliminated, as there is created better vibratory forces through the system."

Treatments included a change in diet, vitamins, a continuation of the medication prescribed by the physician, relaxation, the use of one of the Cayce-prescribed electrical appliances, and the suggestion to refrain from spending too much time on his feet. The man was advised that he was exerting himself too much, both physically and mentally.

One month later, the businessman was apparently healed and feeling well enough to return to his normal schedule, as he wrote Mr. Cayce from Chicago while on a business trip: "I arrived on Sunday, I feel fine, except I get tired and sleepy and a little backache occasionally . . . God is good and just. His greatest blessing to me was the friendship he gave to you and me, and I hope we shall continue to enjoy His blessings together."

A reading that specifically discussed how vibrations might be used to facilitate healing is the case of a forty-four-year-old woman with fibroid breast tumors. Edgar Cayce told her that by beginning a course of treatment immediately and by changing the vibration within her body, it would be possible to completely eradicate the tumors without surgery: ". . . as we find, if the vibrations are raised sufficiently these [tumors] may be dissipated, and—with the body kept in a *constructive* way and manner—eliminated entirely from the system." (683-3)

Her recommended course of treatment included physiotherapy, massage, the use of one of the electrical appliances, and a change in diet. For several days she was encouraged to eat nothing but concord grapes as a means of helping to eliminate toxins from her system. Afterward, she was encouraged to refrain from eating red meat and instead to follow a diet consisting of fish or fowl but principally vegetables and nuts. When she asked if breast surgery would be necessary, Cayce replied that as long as the recommendations were followed, no surgery would be required; however, without following the recommendations, in all likelihood it would become a necessity.

Demonstrating how some of the health recommendations in the

readings continue to be helpful long after Cayce's death, forty years later a woman read about this case and used some of the recommended treatments as her own. She also incorporated the use of castor oil packs—flannel cloth saturated with castor oil—as the readings recommended these packs as a means of helping the body's vibratory forces and enabling the elimination processes to absorb tumors. She reported her experience:

> **The story [of the forty-four-year-old woman with fibroid breast tumors] was very significant for me because I had an experience similar to that woman. I too had discovered a lump in my breast and was told to see a surgeon as soon as possible. My doctor told me he thought it was a cyst and not a tumor but in any event should be removed.**
>
> **I had read where Castor Oil Packs on external cysts, warts and moles were beneficial but I hadn't read where it was recommended for the breast. Well I applied the packs faithfully for about a week. I even fell asleep once with a pack on! Almost immediately the size of the lump decreased.**
>
> **During this time I meditated daily. I say this only because I often miss a day or two and I know meditation has a healing effect on the body.**
>
> **During the next month I continued the packs but only once every two days.**
>
> **It is now two months later since finding the lump and it has disappeared. I returned to my doctor and after examining me found everything normal. He asked if I saw the surgeon and I replied, "no" . . . Whatever–the lump is gone and I feel the Castor Oil had a lot to do with it.   683-3 Reports**

Other situations from the Cayce files that explore the topic of vibrations and healing include the following.

During a reading given to parents of a thirteen–year–old girl who suffered from cramps and menstrual irregularities resulting from a kidney infection, there was the confirmation given that each individual possesses a unique vibration. The parents were told that the medicines that had been recommended by the reading would work in concert with their daughter's specific vibration: "There is a vibratory rate of each individual entity. All properties given as medicinal or active influences upon the circulation or the glandular system respond to those vibrations." (2084-10)

A sixty-five-year-old woman was told that she possessed an innate talent with spiritual and magnetic healing and could, in fact, use that talent to help individuals heal with the vibrations from her hands. (5277-1)

One woman was told that the yogic breathing exercises she had learned could be very beneficial in improving her overall health as well as in enabling each organ of her body to function properly and give off the correct vibration. (283-1)

A fifty-one-year-old woman with a catarrh—an inflammation of the mucous membranes—was told that her condition had come about as an aftereffect of surgery for a partial hysterectomy. Cayce prescribed osteopathic manipulation, electrotherapy, and internal medications that the reading stated would assist "the vibratory forces." She also suffered from general debilitation and backache. Cayce assured her that her health would return by following the recommended treatments. This is how he described her overall condition and prognosis:

> **. . . the mucus force, as has been described, has become clogged, as from the catarrhal condition produced in mucus portions of the system. Breaking up of these, through those properties as we have given, and the correction of impulses from nervous system, and the electrical vibration to change the effect of nerve and blood supply, will remove these conditions from the system.   5654-1**

On another occasion, Cayce recommended a total hysterectomy to a woman who complained of mental problems and psychological aberrations that were causing her a great deal of concern. The reading suggested that it was apparently a hormonal problem that was traceable to her ancestry and heredity. After the surgery, the reading recommended deep massage and vibrational healing that would occur with osteopathic adjustments. The reading ended by stating, "To gain assistance for the body and ease and rest, and to rid it of the hallucinations, do as we have said." (4285-1)

A twenty-five-year-old woman challenged with a number of problems, including what she called an "impure complexion," was given a diet that Cayce claimed would help her eliminations through the intestinal tract and raise "the vibratory forces within the body." A similar diet was recommended for many individuals who received readings for a variety of conditions:

> **Mornings–citrus fruit juices *or* cereals, but not both at the same meal. At other meals there may be taken, or included with the others at times, dried fruits or figs, combined with dates and raisins–these chopped very well together. And for this especial body, dates, figs (that are dried) cooked with a little corn meal (a very little sprinkled in), then this taken with milk, should be almost a spiritual food for the body; whether it's taken one, two, three or four meals a day . . .**
>
> **Noons–such as vegetable juices, or combined with a little meat juices and a combination of raw vegetables; but not *ever* any acetic acid or vinegar or the like with same–but oils, if olive oil or vegetable oils, may be used with same.**
>
> **Evenings–vegetables that are of the leafy nature; fish, fowl or lamb preferably as the meats or their combinations. These of course are not to be all, but this is the *general* outline for the three meals for the body. 275-45**

To be sure, sometimes, in spite of Cayce's recommendations, individuals were not always able or willing to carry out the necessary treatments to regain their health. A case in point is that of a forty-nine-year-old contractor who had apparently fractured his ribs and breastbone in an accident. Although the fracture had occurred sometime previously and the bones had healed with time, the man remained ill. His complaints included dizziness, pains in his abdomen, indigestion, and a burning throat. Sometimes the pains were so acute that he was forced to take a sedative. A reading was obtained in which Cayce traced all of the problems to the aftereffects of the original fracture. In fact, the reading suggested that some of the injured bone had caused an ongoing irritation in the body that had eventually caused problems with the digestive system and the transverse and descending colons. Because of the thickening of the body's tissues, the blood supply had also been affected, resulting in a decrease in the man's energy and vitality.

Recommendations included massage, dietary measures that were designed to ease the individual's difficulties with digestion, an intestinal antiseptic, enemas, and Epsom salts baths. In spite of the long-standing nature of the condition, Mr. (5647) began to recuperate. Unfortunately, however, a complete healing was never obtained. Eight years later, Edgar Cayce's son Hugh Lynn wrote a Mr. J.B. Henning, one of the contractor's friends who had been present for the reading. Hugh Lynn asked for follow-up information on the case. In response, Mr. Henning submitted this report:

> This reading was requested by me and Mr. [4762] as friends of Mr. [5647], who had been ill for some time. We were present for the reading and gave an address in the county where we thought Mr. [5647] was located. When the reading began it was indicated that he was not at the address given. I then suggested another address, and the information indicated that he was located there.
>
> An injury to the ribs was indicated, and I remember when Mr. [5647] received this injury as I was with him at the time. He began to follow the suggestion given and improved rapidly until he reported to me that he was ready to go back to work and asked if I could find him a job.
>
> At this point, he had considerable domestic trouble. His wife left him and for a time he stopped his medicine and diet which was recommended. He became ill again and at my suggestion, later began his treatments. He began to improve again and then, because of domestic troubles, lost interest in living. He discontinued all treatments and soon became critically ill and passed on.
>
> I believe that if he had followed the suggestions thoroughly that he would certainly have improved. It was so evident as long as he followed the suggestions in the reading.
> [signed] J. B. Henning, 14 St & Med. Ave., Va. Beach, Va.
> **5647-1 Reports**

A more favorable outcome dealing with vibrations and health occurred in countless cases in the Cayce files, including that of a thirteen-year-old boy whose parents presented him for a reading in 1930. Their son's problem was obesity; a reading suggested that part of the problem was that his digestive process was "almost too good" and had the effect of turning most foods to sugar. A glandular imbalance had also affected the youth's height and caused him to be under-developed in his gonads. Overall, Cayce recommended that "a necessary change of the vibratory forces is needed for the body . . ." That change in vibratory forces was accomplished through dietary changes, exercise, and vibrational healing. Over a period of eight months, the parents checked the outlook for their son's condition with several additional readings.

The first follow-up report was filed by the boy's mother just a few weeks after the first reading: "Dr. Mayer, our family physician, made up a diet list according to your reading and he was so impressed with the accuracy of the reading . . . Dr. Mayer said the diagnosis was the most remarkable picture of [5603] and that you might have just come from an examination of him." (5603-1 Reports)

Another report was filed by Edgar Cayce's secretary, Gladys Davis: "His parents got the five readings for him, over a period of eight months. In that time his weight went down to normal and he was pronounced cured. His parents were very appreciative and made a large contribution to the Cayce Hospital . . ."

After the vibrational changes had taken place, the youth began to grow and develop normally. His weight and height became normal. In time, the boy reached 5 feet 11 inches and was described as being "slim" at 151 pounds. His mother characterized him as being "most beautifully developed . . . He's so conscientious about his choice of foods—and we owe it all to you!"

Repeatedly, the Edgar Cayce readings connected the health of the physical body and each of its organs to balanced vibrations. In addition to the fact that healing was often facilitated by enabling the body to help heal itself, a number of Cayce treatment modalities emphasized the importance of the vibrations that the modality used in assisting the healing process. Ultimately, however, the readings contend that regardless of the healing modality or treatment, every form of healing is essentially connected to attuning the forces within the body to their balanced state and an awareness of their connection to the divine. As one chiropractor was told, "For ye know deep in thyself that all healing comes of the Lord, and there is not anything you may do save attune the body forces to the very vibration of the body itself to the awareness that God is, and is creative in its every purpose." (3042-1) With this in mind, at a very basic level there is an inextricable connection between vibration and consciousness.

VIBRATIONS
Vibrations and Consciousness

Healing others is healing self. For, to give out that which aids others in reaching that which creates the perfect vibration of life in their physical selves, through the mental attitudes and aptitudes of the body, brings to self better understanding. Yes, in healing others one heals self.   281-18

In December 1933, during the course of a reading on the topic of awakening psychic abilities, a twenty–three–year–old student of electrical engineering asked a question of Edgar Cayce that seemed straightforward enough: "What is the highest possible psychic realization—etc.?" The answer given by the readings, however, might have been very different than the young man had expected, as Cayce replied: "That God, the Father, speaks directly to the sons of men—even as He has promised." (440-4) Interestingly enough, this very premise lies at the heart of the Edgar Cayce information on consciousness development, soul growth, and the highest vibration that is accessible in the earth.

Over the next couple of days, the young man obtained additional readings, including one in which he asked about the best method for developing his own psychic abilities. Cayce advised him that the best approach took into account the fact that psychic ability is a natural byproduct of soul development and spiritual growth. As stated previously, the Cayce cosmology contends that the ultimate goal of each soul is to awaken to an awareness of its oneness with God and its connection to the rest of creation. That awakening occurs through attunement, through application, and through the process of setting spiritual ideals that enable individuals to move beyond the vibration of their present state of consciousness to a higher level. This very concept of how individual consciousness changes as soul growth occurs is essentially referred to by the Apostle Paul in the New Testament, in his First Epistle to the Corinthians: "When I was a child, I spake as a child, I understood as a child, I thought as a child: but when I became a man, I put away childish things." (1 Corinthians 13:11)

The readings contend that all individuals are by birthright "co-creators" with the divine in terms of their capacity to shape their lives and the world in which they live. This co-creative ability is a reality regardless of whether or not individuals become aware of their connection to spirit or even the ultimate purpose for which they came into the earth. However, as individuals are able to raise their consciousness and attune to higher levels of vibration, they can become more perfect channels for the divine will, transforming themselves and those around them in the process. In fact, the readings suggest that rather than thinking that spiritual growth is a means to escape the earth and return to an awareness of our divine origins, it's more appropriate to understand that as we raise our consciousness and vibrations, we literally bring spirit into the earth, transforming the material world in the process.

Obviously, this co-creative capacity possessed by each individual is limited by personal consciousness and the corresponding level of her or his vibration. An example pointed out by the Cayce readings is the Old Testament story of Isaac and Rebekah, and the birth of their twin sons, Esau and Jacob. (Genesis 24–27)

The readings present the story of Isaac and Rebekah as an illustration of two souls who possessed two very different levels of consciousness, and yet each had a co-creative impact upon the child that was attracted into the earth. Cayce states that the differing spiritual ideals and personal desires exemplified by Isaac and Rebekah began at conception and lasted throughout Rebekah's pregnancy, resulting in the outcome that "*both* attitudes found expression." According to the Old Testament, even from birth the twins were very different from one another. Isaac's ideals had attracted Esau, who loved the outdoors and the tracking of game, and was always his father's favorite. Conversely, Rebekah's ideals had created a high enough vibration to attract Jacob, who would grow to become the spiritual father and leader of the nation of Israel. Cayce describes these differences between the brothers:

> **Though conceived at once, born together, they were far separated in their purposes, their aims, their hopes; one holding to that which made body, mind and soul coordinant; the other satisfying, gratifying the appetites of the physical and mental without coordinating same through its spiritual relationships . . .**
> **Do ye think that one received a different instruction from the other? Each received the same, yet their reaction, their choice of that in the environment made physical characteristics that varied in their activity.** 281-48

This account obviously demonstrates just one of the many ways in which co-creation, consciousness, and vibration have an impact upon the material world.

In an effort to more fully understand the co-creative birthright of each and every soul and to outline the steps necessary for raising individual vibration and transforming personal consciousness, Edgar Cayce began giving readings on the subject as he discussed the topic of soul development. These readings were given to individuals interested in personally applying spiritual principles in their everyday lives as a means of committing to soul growth. Eventually, two types of group readings would occur. The first type is often referred to as the

"262 series" and were readings given to the first study group, Norfolk #1. The second type has been called the "281 series" and were readings given to the Glad Helpers Prayer Group. Just as an aside, many of the individuals in the prayer group were the very same people involved in Norfolk #1.

Norfolk #1 began with seventeen individuals who wanted to meet regularly as a group and study Edgar Cayce's work. Some members of the group wanted to become more psychic themselves. Others hoped to become more spiritual, helping their families and the world at large. Cayce connected psychic ability and spiritual development by stating that the first was actually a byproduct of the second and that the ultimate psychic experience was the result of spiritual growth and attunement. The group readings on soul development began, and Cayce encouraged them by advising that if the lessons were applied, each member of the group would be able to "present a light to a waiting world." (262-2)

Instead of receiving a series of simple and straightforward readings on spiritual knowledge and information, for the next eleven years members of Norfolk #1 committed themselves to lessons in soul growth that had to be applied, understood, and lived before Cayce would give them the next subject for their lesson. On another occasion, Cayce advised a twenty–nine–year–old Jewish businessman that the universe demanded a process of development that enabled an individual to become at one with the Creator:

> **For, without passing through each and every stage of development, there is not the correct vibration to become one with the Creator, beginning with the first vibration, as is of the spirit quickened with the flesh, and made manifest in material world (earth's plane).**   **900-16**

Although in this instance Cayce was actually talking about expanding consciousness in dimensions beyond the material world, it is interesting to ponder the notion that there may be a natural pattern of spiritual and consciousness progression contained within every dimension of creation. After all, the study group did receive a sequential step of twelve lessons in spiritual growth—each one having to be applied and understood before the next one was given.

Norfolk #1 worked with spiritual ideals, attunement through daily meditation and prayer, and the personal application of the concepts the group members were studying. Eventually, the group compiled their experiences and their understanding of twelve lessons in spiritual growth as *A Search for God, Book I*. A second set of twelve lessons (*A Search for God, Book II*) eventually followed, exploring a higher octave of very similar principles. The first twelve lessons and a brief overview of each lesson's meaning follows:

I. *Cooperation*: Cooperation is essentially the ability to set aside all personal agendas so that the individual can become a "channel of blessings" to others.

II. *Know Thyself*: This lesson emphasizes the spiritual nature of the soul and the necessity of calling forth from within the godlike qualities that are a part of the soul-self.

III. *What is My Ideal?*: This lesson explores the importance of choosing spiritual ideals as a means of properly motivating one's life in more positive directions.

IV. *Faith*: True faith is an awareness that allows the energy of spirit to work through each individual in spite of any personal shortcomings or imperfections.

V. *Virtue and Understanding*: Virtue is essentially living up to the best that an individual knows to do, whereas understanding is knowledge that has been applied.

VI. *Fellowship*: Fellowship is about creating community and growing in the realization of our connection with one another and our joint connection with the divine.

VII. *Patience*: Patience is about becoming consciously aware of self and all impelling influences in a situation and then striving to offer one's very best in return.

VIII. *The Open Door*: There is a pattern of perfection within each soul that is simply waiting to be awakened by the human will.

IX. *In His Presence*: Even though we are always in God's presence, we forget to open ourselves to the ongoing awareness that He is always in ours.

X. *The Cross and the Crown*: This lesson explores how each soul must meet itself as a means of overcoming habit patterns or desires before becoming aware of its true spiritual nature.

XI. *The Lord Thy God is One*: The readings contend that there is only one force in the universe and that force is God—everything (and everyone) is a part of that force.

XII. *Love*: Love is the best expression of that one universal force. From Cayce's perspective, the primary purpose of life is to let the love of God flow through us.

Early on in the group's experience, Edgar Cayce had a dream in which he was apparently "testing" and "raising" the vibrations of each group member. When a reading was sought on interpreting the dream, Cayce stated that it was a symbolic representation of each individual's experience with the spiritual growth material. In the process of spiritual awakening, each person was becoming aware of the fact that she or he was measuring themselves by the vibration and activities of her or his life. This was the testing by which each member of the group was becoming aware of personal awakening. (262-6)

The readings discuss the fact that the physical body is essentially a reflection of the ideals, desires, and spiritual awareness being worked with by the individual. Ultimately, each person possesses a physical body, a mental "body," and a spiritual "body"—the physical and mental bodies being essentially a shadow of the spiritual vibration. With this in mind, the Cayce information on spiritual growth addresses the importance of working with physical, mental, and spiritual ideals as well as personal application addressing each component. It is for this reason that members of Norfolk #1 included the following when compiling their experiences with the study group readings: "Each . . . entity is a miniature copy of the universe, possessing a physical body, a mental body and a spiritual body. These bodies are so closely associated and related that the vibrations of one affect the other two." (262-10)

Eventually, members of the group inquired about the possibility of raising consciousness to such an extent as to have direct communication with the divine. Cayce replied that it required raising personal vibration to an extremely elevated level; otherwise, the individual would not even be capable of receiving that vibration. Along similar lines, Norfolk #1 inquired why Jesus had told Mary Magdalene not to touch Him immediately after His resurrection. (John 20) The reason discussed by the readings was that Jesus had elevated His entire vibration to such an extreme level that touching Him at that point would have caused electrocution to anyone not vibrating at the same level. In the language of the readings:

> **For the vibrations to which the glorified body was raised would have been the same as a physical body touching a high power current. Why do you say not touch the wire? If ye are in accord, or not in touch with the earth, it doesn't harm; otherwise, it's too bad!**   **262-87**

Almost two years after the group's beginning, Mrs. Frances Morrow, one of the members of Norfolk #1, was asked to give a lecture in which she discussed some of the things group members had learned by studying the material. Her lecture included the following:

> **During these two years through the inspiration and help derived through meditation and prayer, we have gotten out a course of lessons that are now being studied by people scattered throughout the United States. From the reports received by those who have made a study of these lessons great good is being received through them. As a group we will find as we review them that we, too, receive renewed strength and understanding of the aims and purposes of the work . . . the group, itself, has grown in knowledge of the laws of vibration, knowledge of the laws of the forces. It has grown in understanding, understanding of the power of prayer, of healing, of love. Not that it has learned all, just a little, but it has grown, advanced, climbed upward. It has learned something of COOPERATION, of SELF, of a true IDEAL, of FAITH, of FELLOWSHIP, of PATIENCE, of VIRTUE AND UNDERSTANDING, of being IN HIS PRESENCE, of opening the DOOR to the voice of the Master, [THE CROSS AND THE CROWN, THE LORD THY GOD IS ONE] and last, but not least, of the Love that passes understanding . . .**
> **262-47 Reports**

Ultimately, these twelve lessons in personal spirituality had a major impact upon members of Norfolk #1 as well as tens of thousands of individuals who would eventually study the same material decades later. Taken together, these lessons offer individuals from all walks of life and religious backgrounds a practical approach to personal transformation and spiritual development. Over the years, both the information and the number of those involved with the material have grown from very humble beginnings to include hundreds of groups around the globe, foreign translations, and a variety of resource materials.[2]

In addition to the series of readings given to Norfolk #1, a second group, the Glad Helpers Prayer Group, obtained readings for themselves. This group was made up of individuals specifically interested in raising their vibrations and consciousness as a means of becoming healing channels to others through prayer and spiritual healing. Over the years, the group received sixty–five readings on topics including meditation, prayer, healing, consciousness development, vibrations, and even a number of readings on interpreting the Book of Revelation. The rationale suggested by the readings for the Book of Revelation was that it was actually a symbolic representation of the internal struggles that take place within an individual as consciousness and soul development take place and personal vibration is raised to a higher level. Although experienced by the Apostle John during his exile on the Isle of Patmos, the readings contend that John's visionary experience is relevant for every individual:

For the visions, the experiences, the names, the churches, the places, the dragons, the cities, all are but emblems of those forces that may war within the individual in its journey through the material, or from the entering into the material manifestation to the entering into the glory, or the awakening in the spirit, in the inter-between, in the borderland, in the shadow.   **281-16**

---

[2] In addition to the original readings given to Norfolk Study Group #1 (the "262 series"), supplemental materials include the *A Search for God* books and companion resources, such as *Your Life: Why It Is the Way It Is and What You Can Do About It* (McArthur), *Edgar Cayce's Twelve Lessons in Personal Spirituality* (Todeschi), and other materials.

In terms of prayer, meditation, attunement, and spiritual healing, the Cayce readings suggest that as individuals attune themselves to higher states of consciousness, they literally raise their personal vibrations in the process. Not only does this raising of vibrations facilitate personal healing, but it enables the individual to become a catalyst of healing for others. The material provided to the Glad Helpers Prayer Group states that once personal vibrations have been raised, healing others may be accomplished through prayer and the laying on of hands. In fact, on one occasion, Cayce told members of the group that with the proper attunement, *"healing of every* kind and nature may be disseminated on the wings of thought . . ."* (281-13)

As the prayer group continued to work with meditation, prayer, and personal attunement, the readings promised that the individuals working with the information would eventually be able to raise the vibration within themselves to "the consciousness of the oneness of individual life with the Universal Consciousness." (281-7) During the same reading, the group asked for more information regarding the universal laws governing vibration. Cayce told those gathered that raising personal vibration was essentially raising the consciousness of the individual to the Christ Consciousness or divine consciousness within. Once that consciousness was raised within self, those same vibrations could be directed to others in the form of healing. The heightened vibrations would essentially raise the vibrations of the individual to whom they were being directed, facilitating healing in the process. While discussing the laws of spiritual healing, Cayce had this to say:

When a body . . . has so attuned or raised its own vibrations sufficiently, it may–by the motion of the spoken word– awaken the activity of the emotions to such an extent as to revivify, resuscitate or to change the rotary force or influence or the atomic forces in the activity of the structural portion . . . [of another] in such a way and manner as to set it again in motion.

Thus does spiritual or psychic influence of body upon body bring healing to *any* individual . . .   **281-24**

When a member of the prayer group asked—"Is it possible to give
any advice as to how an individual may raise his own vibrations, or
whatever may be necessary, to effect a self-cure?"—the response came:

> By raising that attunement of self to the spirit within, that is
> of the soul–body–about which we have been speaking . . .
> *Who* hath given thee power? Within what live ye? *What* is
> Life? Is it the *attuning* of self, then, to same. *How?*
> As the body-physical is purified, as the mental body is
> made wholly at-one with purification or purity, with the
> life and light within itself, healing comes, strength comes,
> power comes.
> So may an individual effect a healing, through meditation,
> through attuning not just a side of the mind nor a portion of
> the body but the whole, to that at-oneness with the spiritual
> forces within, the gift of the life-force within each body.
> For . . . when matter comes into being, what has taken
> place? The Spirit ye worship as God has *moved* in space and
> in time to make for that which gives its expression; perhaps
> as wheat, as corn, as flesh, as whatever may be the
> movement in that ye call time and space.
> Then *making* self in an at-onement with that Creative
> Force brings what? That necessary for the activity which has
> been set in motion and has become manifested to be in
> accord *with* that First Cause.   281-24

The readings used an example from Scripture to illustrate how
healing was made possible through individuals that had made
themselves in attunement with the divine consciousness—becoming
channels of healing in the process. In the story, the Apostles John and
Peter were heading toward the temple to pray. On their way they
encountered a man who was crippled from birth, begging for money.
Peter told the cripple that although they had no money, they could
offer healing: "Silver and gold have I none, but such as I have I give
thee. In the name of Jesus Christ of Nazareth rise up and walk." (Acts 3:6)
Immediately the man was healed; he rose, walked, and leapt for joy.
That healing, Cayce suggested, had been possible because both Peter

and John had raised their consciousness and vibrations to such an extent that they could impact the vibrations of others. Cayce told the group:

> Vibration, to be sure, is an enormous subject, and while all may not wholly understand that which is accomplished through the raising of vibration in self, the directing of vibration to others, these may aid with that sincerity that comes with the closer walk with those Creative Forces . . .
>
> Vibration is, in its simple essence or word, *raising* the Christ Consciousness in self to such an extent as it may flow *out* of self to him thou would direct it to. As, "Silver and gold I have none, but such as I have give I unto thee." "In the *name* of Jesus Christ, stand up and walk!" *That* is an illustration of vibration that heals, manifested in a material world. What flowed out of Peter and John? That as received by knowing self in its entirety, body, mind, soul, is one *with* that Creative Energy that is *life* itself!   281-7

During a reading independent of the prayer group, Cayce told an individual seeking help for a glandular imbalance that it would be beneficial to read the Book of Revelation and try to understand the Revelation especially in relationship to what was occurring within the individual's mind and body. Cayce suggested that the Revelation provided an illustration of what transpired within an individual as he or she evolved in consciousness. (2501-7)

Drawing upon the connection between the physical body, consciousness growth and attunement, and the symbolism of Revelation, for ten years (1933-1943) members of the Glad Helpers Prayer Group explored an interpretation of the Book of Revelation in greater detail with Edgar Cayce. The readings contend that the seven churches are symbolic of the seven spiritual centers, or chakras, within the body (gonads, leyden, adrenals, thymus, thyroid, pineal, and pituitary) and that the four beasts correspond to the four lower centers. Other connections between the Revelation and the individual include the fact that the four and twenty elders mentioned within the text are associated with the twenty-four cranial nerves that control the five senses of the body and that the red dragon's seven heads and ten horns are symbolic of the rebellious forces within self that would attempt to destroy a higher spiritual ideal.[3]

Overall, the readings suggest that one of the most helpful ways to explore the Book of Revelation is one of archetypal, or universal, symbolism. Through a series of images and pictures, the Revelation portrays a sequential process that corresponds to the awakening of the higher self. It depicts the internal struggles that occur within each individual as spiritual development takes place and the basic lower nature of humankind evolves to its higher spiritual nature. In simplest terms, the Revelation is essentially a handbook for the sequential evolution of human consciousness as individuals reawaken to their connection to the divine.

At one point, longtime Cayce scholar and author Herbert Bruce Puryear outlined a seven-step process that explored the twenty-two chapters of Revelation and the Glad Helpers Prayer Group's understanding:

I.   Revelation 1-4: Addresses the Seven Churches of the Revelation and essentially corresponds to the activity and process of self-evaluation.

II. Revelation 5-8: Opening the Seven-Sealed book is connected to the process of opening the seven spiritual centers within the body.

III. Revelation 9-11: Sounding the Seven Trumpets is about personal purification.

IV. Revelation 12-14: The appearance of the seven characters is associated with the establishment of the Higher Self as the Ideal.

V.   Revelation 15-16: The Seven Angels with Seven Vials is connected with an individual meeting the karmic memory contained within each of the seven centers.

VI. Revelation 17-20: The Fall of Babylon is about overthrowing the dominion of the lower self.

VII. Revelation 21-22: Obviously, a New Heaven and a New Earth corresponds to the ascendancy of the higher self.

---

[3] For an in-depth exploration of this topic, see *Soul Signs* (Todeschi).

The Cayce approach to the Revelation sees the imagery of the text as, first and foremost, a symbolic look at what occurs within individuals as attunement takes place and personal vibration is raised to a higher level. It was for that reason that the prayer group undertook an exploration of this material in the first place.

Ultimately, the readings obtained by both the Norfolk #1 Study Group and the Glad Helpers Prayer Group essentially consist of information about attaining the universal Christ Consciousness. Rather than being connected to religious dogma, these materials are about the spiritual development possible for every soul in the earth, regardless of religion. In fact, from Cayce's perspective, Jesus became the pattern for spiritual attainment relevant for every religion. His life example is about attuning to the divine within so that the Self can become a conduit for spiritual vibrations and healing in the material world. For this reason, when one member of the prayer group asked for a personal affirmation that could be sent to and used by those who had asked for spiritual healing, the following was suggested: *There is being raised within me that Christ Consciousness that is sufficient for every need within my body, my mind, my soul.* (281-7)

The readings provide practical guidance for daily application of spiritual principles in the earth. As these principles are applied, soul growth and the elevation of personal vibration become the natural result. In time, that personal growth affects the individual, enabling the individual to be more in tune with divine consciousness. This growth in consciousness and vibration ultimately affects the world at large. With this in mind, on one occasion, the readings gently encouraged members of the prayer group to keep working with the material. The advice they received is relevant for any individual interested in the topic of vibrations and consciousness:

Keep in that way, in patience, in persistence, in sincerity, in truth. Faint not that there are periods when apparently little is seen to be accomplished externally. Know that thou hast set in motion that leaven that worketh all unseen, yet will bring the consciousness of His love, His hope, His presence, into the lives of all. Each should be patient first with self, in

honor preferring one another. Sit not in the seat of the scornful. Stand not in the place of the cynic. Be mindful not of things of high estate; rather give place to that that makes for sweetening in the lives of all; for he that wishes his brother well, yet makes no move to aid or supply, or to comfort, or to cheer, is only fooling self. He that would know the way must be oft in prayer, joyous prayer, *knowing* He giveth life to as many as seek in sincerity to be the channel of blessing to someone; for "Inasmuch as ye did a kindness, a holy word, a clothing in act as to one of these the least of my little ones, ye have done it unto me." As He knoweth thee, so may ye know Him, ye who have been chosen for the various channels of activity in spirit, in mind, in body, for the manifesting of His glory in the earth. Be faithful. Do not allow self to be so overcome in *any* manner as to miss that calling in Him; for He is faithful who has promised to be near.

We are through.   281-12

VIBRATIONS
Vibrations and Location

For, each state, each town, each city, each community is made up of the choice of groups or masses that give expression to creative influences—whether of a social, political or economic nature. For these, too, have their influence by the manner of expression of the individual entities who make the whole.   2571-1

IN 1932, EDGAR CAYCE had two dream experiences that seemed to emphasize the connection between vibrations and specific locations. Although readings connecting vibrations with certain places had occurred previously, these two dreams prompted Cayce to seek firsthand additional information on the topic. The first dream occurred about five months after the Norfolk #1 Study Group had started to meet and had begun to work with the spiritual growth information presented in the readings. The second dream occurred three months after the first and portrayed Edgar Cayce traveling around the country and meeting with various individuals from the Norfolk #1 group.

In the first dream, Edgar Cayce saw himself as a speck of light or a grain of sand. From this tiny point, he suddenly seemed to radiate upward, like a spiral or a whirlwind. As he rose higher, the spirals became larger, encompassing broader reaches of space. The movement became a continuous motion that appeared to create an enormous funnel opening up into infinity. When a reading was obtained to interpret this portion of the dream, the sleeping Cayce replied, "As indicated, the entity is—in the affairs of the world—a tiny speck, as it were, a mere grain of sand; yet when raised in the atmosphere or realm of the spiritual forces it becomes all inclusive, as is seen by the size of the funnel . . ." (294-131)

While Cayce was having the dream and perceiving himself as traveling higher through these ever-expanding spirals, he became aware of the various kinds of energies that seemed to be radiating from different areas of the country. Each of these energies was associated with different types of vibrations. For example, one area or city seemed to be radiating a vibration that was associated with health or healing, while another seemed to be more closely aligned with commerce. In the midst of the dream, Cayce realized that it would be much easier for him to give a health reading in a city that emanated the health vibration than it would be to give the same reading elsewhere, when that vibration was not present. He also understood that some cities and the energies they emitted were at a much higher vibration than others were. He then made note of the fact that (at that time—1932) the vibrations of a city like Rochester, New York, appeared to be at a higher frequency than the overall vibrations of a place like Chicago, Illinois.

When a reading later explored this portion of Cayce's dream, the response came that the imagery presented the fact that although individuals could receive healing wherever they were located, the vibration of a person's specific locale could not help but influence the overall "tone" of the healing received. The reading also stated that individuals, groups, classes, masses, and even nations, through their collective activities, "create their position [and their corresponding vibration] in the affairs of the universe." (294-131)

Again, the second dream took place in April 1932 and depicted Edgar

Cayce traveling to various portions of the country and meeting with members of the Norfolk #1 Study Group. At every location, as he stopped to meet with a member of the group, Cayce presented a package to that individual—a package that was apparently a compilation of spiritual truths which were supposed to be disseminated by that specific group member to that area of the country.

When a reading was requested to interpret this dream, Cayce replied that it was a vision depicting where each group member would find a receptive audience for disseminating the spiritual truths she or he had begun studying. Apparently, each person within the group possessed a vibration that was more in keeping with working within the area of the country that had been depicted in the dream.

Intrigued by the information, members of the group asked the sleeping Cayce to describe where each had been when they received their particular package. That portion of the reading follows (Note: Each member of the group is identified by his or her respective reading number):

(Q) In what particular portion of the country was [69], and what is the message?
(A) In the middle west, or in Denver, as was seen. There the aid may be the greater as presented by the body. The message, that as compiled by all seen.
(Q) [307]:
(A) Was in that of Cleveland, or that portion of the country, and in the presentation as of studying, or as presenting in the logic of same.
(Q) [993]:
(A) In the southland, or New Orleans, as seen, and among such groups may the body present the greater message.
(Q) [560]:
(A) In Kentucky and Tennessee, that portion where the studies of same have been for many the day as those of the *orthodox* forces, or church ritualistic forces. These will be hard; but truth prevails!
(Q) [404]:
(A) These presented in the eastern portion and northern

portion of the country, as of southern New England, among those especially of the spiritual faith.

(Q) [413]:

(A) These were in the eastern portion of the south, and in that of southern Georgia and Florida, but as in the peach orchard section.

(Q) [341]:

(A) These presented more in the far west.

(Q) [295]:

(A) In the southwest, or San Antonio and that portion of the country, and among those of the particular sect or sets of people.

(Q) [303]:

(A) These were in the Carolinas, and especially that portion about those of the student body, or peoples.

(Q) [585]:

(A) This was seen in those of the valley country of West Virginia, or the northwestern portion of that part of the country, and as the travel indicated there, in that that pertained most to the waterways.

(Q) [379]:

(A) These were in Oklahoma, and those portions of southern part of Missouri, or–as what would be called–in the Ozark portion of the country.

(Q) [115]:

(A) Among those of the southwestern portion, and especially of that as pertained to those of the cult natures.

(Q) Mrs. [69]'s husband:

(A) Those of the harder headed portions, in the north and northwestern portions of Texas.

(Q) [288]:

(A) In that portion of the northeastern portion of the country, as in the vinelands of New York.

(Q) [2112]:

(A) In Indiana and Illinois, or as to that portion in which there is seen those of a peculiar peoples, as termed by many. Most of them holding to that of folklore, or of the Zionists.

(Q) [2125]:
(A) Among the peoples at home! [Virginia]
(Q) [2124]:
(A) In that portion of the southwest, as in Arizona and New Mexico, especially in that portion among the miner and the rodeo peoples.
(Q) [2673]:
(A) She in that portion now called the far northwest, as in Oregon, Washington, and that portion of the land.
  Well that these be understood, that that portion of the lessons as are compiled in the whole will be most *appealing* to that section from these of the group seen.
  We are through.   262-16

Years later, Gladys Davis Turner placed a notation in the files about this particular dream. Gladys had been Cayce's secretary as well as a member of Norfolk #1. Gladys had the following to say: "In several instances this reading has proven true. As study group work grew throughout the country, there developed a strange rapport and response between the different areas and the individual 'assigned' to that area . . ." (262-16 Reports) In terms of the accuracy of the information for Gladys, herself, Cayce's dream had connected Gladys with "that portion of the country, as in the vinelands of New York." In 1945, a couple of months after Edgar Cayce's death, Gladys wrote a friend about an experience she had had while visiting New York to discuss the Cayce work:

> I sure did get my visit to N.Y. in at the right time, didn't I. Elenor [Elenor S. Cooley] was right when she said everything was "set" for it and that I couldn't help myself. I got a berth going and coming, the last one on the coach each time, and without making a reservation ahead of time. Not seeing you again before I left I didn't get to tell you about a dream I had while at Mr. Kurtz [Matthew J. and Margaret G. Kurtz] home. I thought I was in the basement stringing up clothes lines from one corner to the other. When I finished I had made a perfect spider web. That's exactly what I did while in N.Y.; every contact led to another and it was almost like I was on a string and couldn't help myself. I finally decided I'd better

come home before I started another spider web–it would have been so easy. This is especially interesting, considering the information in a reading years ago. Mr. Cayce had a dream regarding the Study Group members [262-16, Par. 21-A], the interpretation of which (in the reading) gave each one the section of the country in which they could have the greater influence or the group which spoke their language. When my name was called, the answer came, "The vine lands of New York." I never knew what it meant by the vine lands until I had that dream about the spider web, after I had been chasing all over N.Y. City, Westchester, Long Island and New Jersey visiting people of such different walks of life yet all connected by the thread of the Ass'n work. (With me as the spider!)

Love, Gladys   1472-13 Reports

The Cayce information suggests that individuals create a personal vibration through their thoughts and activities. In fact, to a group of individuals studying Cayce's psychic work, Edgar Cayce suggested that the reason Jesus had once told an audience that thinking about adultery was the same as committing it was because thoughts created the same vibration as acting out those thoughts. In other words, the individual's entire being—physically, mentally, and spiritually—was just as affected by the thoughts that person held in mind as she or he was by the actions that individual carried out. Here is the account from the New Testament:

Ye have heard that it was said by them of old time, Thou shalt not commit adultery:

But I say unto you, That whosoever looketh on a woman to lust after her hath committed adultery with her already in his heart.   Matthew 5:27-28

The readings affirm that thoughts build the same energetic vibration as the activity: "Whenever it vibrates in the *same* vibration, it shows as the same thing . . . Now here we have the relativity of force as applied through the mental body . . . taking thought, or building by the mental body . . ." (254–47) Cayce advised those gathered that depending on the nature of that held in mind, every thought "contributed or detracted" to the soul growth of the individual.

The collective vibrations of individuals in a particular place or location combine together to then create an energy or vibration all its own. The vibration of that location, in turn, radiates outward to attract others resonating at the very same level. For this reason it is not a stretch of the imagination to understand how crime can spread throughout a city in the same manner that individuals meditating in a particular location have been statistically proven to bring peace and calm to that same locale. Somehow activities of a group of people have a leavening effect vibrationally upon an area. The concept of vibrations and how they work in terms of location is contained in a variety of readings excerpts from the Cayce archives, including the following.

During the course of a Life reading given to a thirty–year–old secretary who had been born in Bokhoma, Oklahoma, Cayce commented that one of the unique factors regarding her birthplace was that the vibration of the area made it very unlikely that individuals who had been born there would ever commit suicide. Discussing the effect of the vibration, he said, "Something in the soil; get it between your toes and you'll never commit suicide." (5125-1)

On another occasion, during a reading given to a sixty–four–year–old astrologer, Cayce commented that his birthplace (Anderson, South Carolina) attracted a very large percentage of souls who would eventually have a level of prominence in society. The reading also discussed how the phenomenon of vibration and location tended to work:

> . . . as has been indicated, each town, each city, has its own vibrations by that which has been builded in the conscious-ness of the groups, of that organization, corporation or the like. Here we have an unusual one. The proportions will be about one in five hundred people born in Anderson, South Carolina that will be world-known . . .   3356-1

While giving a physical reading for a fifty–eight–year–old woman who was suffering from hypertension and arteriosclerosis and was located in a place different from where the reading was being given, Cayce commented that even her house had apparently taken on the vibration of the woman's problems:

Yes, taking the conditions of this body, [664] as we have here, as a pattern or example, much might be pointed out as to how the environs of a place, house, room or surroundings are changed or produced by the dwelling there of an individual that radiates even distressed conditions from itself.   **664-1**

In a similar vein, a physical reading was obtained by an individual who had requested help and had agreed to be at work during the time of the reading, providing Edgar Cayce with her physical address as a means of tuning in to her at the time of the reading. However, when the reading began, Cayce apparently did not find the individual there. A follow-up report suggested that she had gone home for lunch. Nonetheless, Cayce was able to obtain the information from the vibrations that surrounded the woman's workplace. (4631-2)

While giving a physical reading to a thirty-nine-year-old man, residing on Bordeaux Street in New Orleans, Louisiana, Cayce discussed the vibration of the area: "Yes, what a peculiar vibration about this place. Many of those things that are often called haunts would like to visit here." (3557-1)

A reading given to a thirty-four-year-old Dictaphone operator recommended that she live in a small town rather than in a congested city. The rationale was that her vibration tended to become confused by the energy of a larger place. Cayce went on to say:

This isn't to imply that the entity is a "small town" body but rather that the entity must in its application of its abilities know its field of activity, its limitations as well as its abilities and then apply them so as to meet the needs to correct those tendencies or weaknesses of the individual entity's ego or individuality.   **3351-1**

When another woman asked how she could best draw the people of the "right vibration" toward her, the response came:

> By the correct vibration in self. Like begets like. Toned to a tone brings the proper tone from the perfect radiation of such. Each entity *radiates* that tone, that reflection of the concept of its creative force. Each entity, each atom of the entity, radiates that vibration to which it attunes itself. Each entity contacts, each entity brings that about itself by putting into action laws, those conditions, those individuals, those vibrations that are necessary for its own development.
> 2842-2

However, when a fifty-five year-old government employee asked what locality would be the best for her in which to vibrate, the response was simply: "Where thou *art!* For the vibrations should be from *within,* rather than from *without!* And so create within thine inner self those closer relationships that where thy body is, *there* may be found succor and aid and help and love for others." (1183-1)

In spite of this suggestion, the readings did state that the vibrations of an area could not help but have a direct impact upon individuals. For example, a woman seeking mental and spiritual counsel during a Cayce reading asked why she felt free of her particular problem only when she was in Pennsylvania. Cayce responded that it was because the vibrations of her being were more in tune with that area of Pennsylvania. The reading went on to describe a similar happening in the life of Jesus:

> Why, ye may ask, did the Master love to be in Galilee, when the house of the Lord His God was in Jerusalem? Why did he love to be alone in the mount? This within the self of this individual entity, and others, brings the vibrations with which it attunes to the variations in soul, mind, body. This is better accomplished in some particular place or position where there may be the same attunement of the vibrations of the body.
> 3357-2

On another occasion, a reading given to a medical doctor confirmed the physician's findings that various medicinal drugs and treatment applications often appeared to have a different response because of the vibration of the environment in which they were administered. (3559-1) From the readings' perspective, the vibrations of a location even have a measurable effect upon the health of individuals residing within that location. For example, in 1943 Cayce told a fifty-five-year-old dentist that the vibrations of a city had an influence upon teeth and cavities so that, for example, those living in New York or Connecticut would not require as much attention to their teeth as those living in Georgia, Tennessee, or Ohio would. (3211-2)

The readings also explored the topic of vibrations in some of the past-life information contained in the Cayce files. For example, parents of a fourteen-year-old girl obtained a Life reading for their daughter as a means of discerning which of the girl's past lives were most influencing her in the present. During the reading, Cayce mentioned that in a previous incarnation the girl had been drawn to the settling of a new land because of the "ideals and principles" that went into the establishment of "the spirit of Virginia." He went on to describe how vibrations were created and how the individuals who were attracted to those vibrations were affected by them:

> **For, each state, each town, each city, each community is made up of the choice of groups or masses that give expression to creative influences–whether of a social, political or economic nature. For these, too, have their influence by the manner of expression of the individual entities who make the whole.   2571-1**

Similarly, a husband and wife obtained a past-life reading and were told that they also had been connected during a Palestine lifetime, at a time when they had been drawn together as a helpful influence toward one another. In attempting to explain how that vibratory attraction worked, the reading used the following analogy:

Did you ever try to analyze why that ye enter some places, some homes which are indeed homes and others, from the very feel, if ye are sensitive at all, there is confusion; there is anger, there is abuse . . . Try this by entering a church and go from there to a jail and then go from the jail into a church–you will find it. So it is with individuals as they have entered earthly experience in various spheres or periods . . .

Those, then, who hold animosity, hold grudges are building for themselves that which they must meet in confusion, in abuse of self, abuse of others, abuse of groups . . . For there must be every type . . . there are even [every imaginable type] in the protestant churches, Methodist, Christian, Baptist, Congregational or the what, but it is to meet the needs . . .

These individuals chose one another as companions. For what? Because they fitted into such companionship, becoming more and more daily as one and as a complement as one, finding in the other that which would answer their needs . . . So it is with these companions, finding in each, as in this experience, that each sought and found that which answers in the present that of prayer, of meditation, of that vibration in each which may be as healing to selves, as hope for others.   2072-15

When a sixty–five–year–old widow asked about the desirability of her returning to Virginia Beach, Cayce told her, "This again as indicated is a matter of choice within self. Here we have those activities of a vibration, that are much in keeping with the intent and purposes of the entity. Hence many harmonious associations and connections might be found in this environ. (1152-9)

A psychologist looking for relocation advice in the pursuit of his career gave Edgar Cayce a series of locations and wondered which would be the best place to carry on his work. Those locations included Clarksburg, West Virginia; London or Hamilton, Ontario; or Davenport, Iowa. Of those mentioned, Cayce recommended Clarksburg, Hamilton, and Davenport because of the effect these cities would have upon the psychologist and his work. He advised against London. He also recommended that the individual look into possibilities along the lakes in Wisconsin, as well as Roanoke and Virginia Beach, Virginia. (4889-1)

On another occasion, when a woman asked Edgar Cayce why Washington, D.C. and Virginia Beach affected her in terms of pressure in her sinuses, Cayce replied that her vibration was higher than those two cities and it manifested in her body as a feeling of pressure. He recommended that she consider instead somewhere in Florida, especially Miami, Palm Beach, or Clearwater. Somehow, these areas were more conducive to her own "vibratory forces." (1318-1)

Even Edgar Cayce himself received relocation advice as a means of making his vibrations and the work he was trying to accomplish more harmonious with the vibrations of the area in which he lived. This was one of the reasons that Virginia Beach, Virginia, had been recommended as the place to establish the Cayce work. At the time, the area was a very small town with only a few hundred people. For all practical purposes the town was a small summer resort that closed down after the end of August. Nonetheless, Cayce's family and his secretary moved to Virginia Beach, but they had a hard time imagining why the readings had brought them to this place. For that reason Cayce's wife and secretary asked the following question during the course of a reading in December 1925: "It has often been given . . . that at or near Virginia Beach, Va., was the place from which this phenomena should be propagated. Will you please tell us (since we are here), in an understandable manner to all present, *why* this is the place . . . ?" (254-26)

Cayce's response was that the location had been recommended for several reasons. One was that the area was open-minded, enabling Cayce's work to expand at some point in the future. Another was that it was near large population centers, specifically the nation's capital, so that it was easily accessible to large groups of people—students, philosophers, theologians, and scientists—who would eventually wish to study the information. However, one of the primary reasons was that the vibrations of Virginia Beach were ideal for Edgar Cayce's psychic ability to operate.

In 1944 Cayce told a fifty-three-year-old man that one of the peculiarities of Columbus, Ohio—his birthplace—was that two very different vibrations seemed to occur in the area and were cyclical in nature. With this in mind, it would be a good place to be born for some and for others not so good—apparently dependent upon which vibration was prominent at the time of birth and how that vibration interacted with the individual's own. (3544-1) Another person was told that one of her strongest innate motivations was the desire for harmony in relationships with others and being around those of a similar vibration and purpose. (2326-1)

A forty-six-year-old housewife learned that souls incarnating into the earth were attracted to the same vibration that they had experienced and created in their previous lifetimes. (757-8) A woman moving into a different apartment mentioned that she did not feel the same degree of spiritual attunement that she had felt in her previous residence. Cayce commented that it was because of the low vibrations that remained as residue by those who had lived in the apartment previously. He recommended continuing to work with her spiritual ideals and "high vibratory influences" (such as meditation and prayer), which would dispel the vibrations of the individuals who had moved. (1472-9)

A thirty-four-year-old factory worker suffering from loneliness was told that she would feel most at home in those vibrations having to do with fame or crowds or locations where emotions had given rise to exciting conditions and activities. (1747-3) A fifty-seven-year-old writer, who was apparently sensitive to the vibrations of a city, was told in her reading that it would be easier for her to describe a city's vibrations than it would be to describe streets or various landmarks. (3420-1)

Other brief comments derived from the readings on the topic of vibrations and location include the following: "Toledo, Ohio—he's in good vibrations!" (3505-1) "Evanston, Wyoming—yes another cycle [cycle of vibration]." (3513-1) "Beaver County—same cycle as Oil City!" (3478-2) "Sivas, Turkey—what a quaint place—a new cycle!" (3908-1) "A new cycle. Pretty high on the vibration [Duluth, Minn.]." (3541-1) "Yes, we have the body here, [3253]—real vibrations about the place here." (3253-1)

In addition to homes, workplaces, cities, towns, and states possessing their own unique vibration, the Edgar Cayce information contends that even nations possess a vibration all their own. In June 1944, at the thirteenth annual membership meeting of the association, Edgar Cayce was asked to give a reading on the topic of vibrations and nations. Part of that discussion included the surprising idea that souls were choosing to be born into certain nations as a means of helping to change the vibration of that nation. The idea was that as the vibration of the nation began to change, more individuals who resonated to the same new cycle would be attracted to the area and eventually the consciousness of the people would change. Cayce commented that these changes were "far off as man counts time, but only a day in the heart of God . . ." (3976–29) Given during the height of the war, the two nations cited for the greatest changes to come were Russia and China. Cayce predicted that China would eventually become the cradle of applied spirituality in the lives of individuals. And, in terms of Russia, the readings suggested that the vibration that was coming was one of "freedom, freedom!—that each man will live for his fellow man!" Whether or not these vibrational changes will manifest or are still in the process of manifesting, only time will tell.

Repeatedly, the Edgar Cayce readings emphasize the fact that each location—from a home or a room to a city or a nation—emanates a vibration that is essentially created by the thoughts and activities of the individuals within that place. Those vibrations put off an energy that resonates to others at the same level. In this way, the readings suggest, the vibrations bring together individuals and activities that resonate with the same energy—much like a tuning fork that is struck can cause another tuning fork nearby to resonate at the very same vibration. It is simply a manifestation of "like attracts like." That energy has a measurable impact upon the location and the people residing within. It is an impact that can be observed even down to the physical level.

VIBRATIONS
Vibrations of Sound, Color, and Stone

Also tones, colors, stones of peculiar type or turn, mean much to the entity. And not as an omen, but for its greater vibration . . . 813-1

I N LARGE PART IT WAS THE WORK of the Glad Helpers Prayer Group that explored the Cayce information on vibrations to discover the variety of ways in which the one force found expression in the material world. Not only did group members discover that vibration is associated with each of the seven spiritual centers and each soul's gradual awakening to higher states of consciousness from within, but the group's efforts expanded to include much more. In addition to exploring the spiritual centers, or chakras, and examining the Revelation and archetypal symbolism, the prayer group delved into the subject of vibrations. In time, the group discovered that the spiritual centers had an affinity with colors, notes, and even motivational impulses, each with its corresponding level of vibration. Eventually, it became clear that everything is vibration, and all of vibration emanates from the one force. Whether it is the faculty of sense perception and the way vibration creates the awareness of such things as sound and color or any of the components of the material world, from the physicality of the human creature to the density of precious stones—all are simply variations of the one force in motion.

The readings encouraged members of the prayer group to explore the information on color and vibration in their daily lives as well as in their meditations. They were told to discern how the colors affected them by seeing whether each color had a "positive" or a "negative" impact upon them through personal experience. Cayce told members of the group:

> **For a reference to these, let each in your study of these, as in relation to the centers themselves, consider the effect of the color itself upon thine own body as ye attempt to apply same by either concentration, dedication or meditating upon these. For as has been given, color is but vibration. Vibration is movement. Movement is activity of a positive and negative force. Is the activity of self as in relationship to these then positive?**   **281-29**

In 1978 much of the information explored by the Glad Helpers Prayer Group was compiled into the *A.R.E. Meditation Course*—an exploration of meditation, prayer, and the physiology of attunement. In terms of the chakras, the endocrine glands, colors, elements, notes, motivational impulses, and their corresponding level of vibration, the following chart adapted from that course may provide an easy reference guide:

Center	Endocrine Gland	Motivational Impulse	Associated Color	Associated Note	Element (if any)
7 highest vibration of the seven centers	Pituitary	Oneness	Violet	Ti	
6	Pineal	Spiritual Perfection	Indigo	La	
5	Thyroid	Will (Divine or self)	Blue	Sol	
4	Thymus	Self–Gratification	Green	Fa	Air
3	Adrenals	Self–Preservation	Yellow	Mi	Fire
2	Cells of Leydig	Sexuality and male/female balance	Orange	Re	Water
1 lowest vibration of the seven centers	Gonads	Survival	Red	Do	Earth

It is important to realize that this table is not meant to contain all of the vibrations that are possible in the earth or does it suggest that any of the categories are complete within themselves. For example, Edgar Cayce once wrote that white was the highest vibration of color: "The perfect color, of course, is white, and this is what we are all striving for. If our souls were in perfect balance then all our color vibrations would blend and we would have an aura of pure white." (Cayce, pg. 14) On another occasion, when recommending school colors for the Cayce-affiliated Atlantic University, the readings suggested purple and gold, as they were manifestations of the "highest" color vibration. (2087-3)

Overall, however, the chart does suggest that there are a variety of vibrational referents for each of the seven spiritual centers, which Cayce saw as points of contact between the physical body and the ultimate spiritual reality of humankind.

During the series of readings given to the prayer group, Cayce also talked about the vibrational quality of chanting and how the musical tones associated with chanting could be helpful in healing and assisting others in attuning to a higher vibration themselves. In fact, Edgar Cayce contended that healing through the use of chants had first been incorporated in the healing temples in ancient Egypt and that the Glad Helpers Prayer Group could continue that effort in their own work with spiritual healing in the present. In 1936, while discussing attunement, breathing, and the power of chanting, the readings recommended the following to the prayer group:

As has been given so oft of old, purge ye your bodies, washing them with water, putting away those things of the mind and of the body; for tomorrow the Lord would speak with thee . . .

So do ye in thy meditation. For thy prayer is as a supplication or a plea to thy superior; yet thy meditation is that thou art meeting on *common* ground!

Then prepare thyself!

In breathing, take into the right nostril, *strength!* Exhale through thy mouth. Intake in thy left nostril, exhaling through the right; opening the centers of thy body–if it is first prepared to thine *own* understanding, thine *own* concept of what *ye* would have if ye would have a visitor, if ye would have a companion, if ye would have thy bridegroom!

Then, as ye begin with the incantation of the [Har-r-r-r-r-aum] Ar-ar-r-r-r–the e-e-e, the o-o-o, the m-m-m, *raise* these in thyself; and ye become close in the presence of thy Maker– as is *shown* in thyself! . . .

For as ye are honest, as ye are patient, as ye are sincere with thyself in thy meeting with thy God, thy Savior, thy Christ, in thy meditation, ye will be in thy dealings with thy fellow man.

We are through for the present.   281-28

One individual who was a member of both the prayer group and the Norfolk #1 Study Group was Esther Wynne. Esther was a fifty-three-year-old high school teacher who took on the task of compiling what would eventually become *A Search for God, Book I.* An immense supporter of the Cayce work, Esther also suggested that a standard question be asked Mr. Cayce during the process of every Life reading—those readings dealing with the subject of reincarnation. That question generally included some variation of the following: "What is my [life] seal, to what color or colors do I best vibrate, and what is my musical note?" Obviously, the question added another group of individuals to the exploration of vibrations who probably would not have inquired about it on their own, providing the Cayce files with supplemental information on the topic.

For example, when a forty-three-year-old bookkeeper with health, financial, relationship, and philosophical questions obtained a reading, she inquired: "To what color or colors does my body vibrate best?" Cayce responded: "To violet. Blue. These are the healing colors for this body." (303-2) When she went on to ask how she could overcome the vibrations of others who were not in "attune" with her own, the reply came: "Filling self's mind (Mind the Builder) with those things that create more and more a unison of *creative* thinking, whether this be as applied to material, spiritual, or purely mental and social relations. Be sure they are *creative* in their essence."

On another occasion, parents of a two-year-old boy who loved to spend time outside were told that in the boy's most recent past-life experience, he had been an Irish priest who had gone westward with settlers, ministering to cowboys, homesteaders, Indians, and others who were in need in the great outdoors. When the question was asked, "To what color, or colors, does the entity best vibrate?" the answer was straightforward: "Those of the somber natures or colors, or especially nature in the spring and fall." (1990-3)

The mother of a fourteen-year-old girl was advised to encourage her daughter to often "wear blue, gold and yellow close to the body." Apparently, the vibration of each of these was more in keeping with the girl's own vibrations. Cayce advised, "These, as colors, as vibrations, will make for the better environment for the body." (3806-1) Similarly, a sixty-three-year-old editor was encouraged to wear the colors "white mauve and shades of purple," as they would create a positive influence and a "helpful vibration" in the woman's daily life. (3395-2)

In the case of a forty-nine-year-old woman with an apparent tendency to be supersensitive toward light, color, or motion, a reading advised her that it was actually the vibration of each of these things that affected her. Apparently, the energy put off by these vibrations caused friction with her own, causing her to feel physically out of balance. (1770-1) Later, the woman was encouraged to work with chanting, making the sound within herself: "O-oooo-ah-m-mmm-u-uuu-r-rrr-n—nn," as the vibration would help to bring greater harmony into her experience. (1770-2)

A thirty-six-year-old restaurateur was told that the color with which she had a vibrational affinity was blue. Cayce went on to state, "And when wearing blue you won't get mad! And make much of these in the underthings, too, close to the body." (594-1) Another woman was also encouraged to wear shades of blue with purple because of the high vibrations associated with the colors. (1554-4) When a fifty-nine-year-old woman asked for advice on what colors or jewelry she should wear "in order to have better vibrations" the readings suggested: "Any of jewelry or ornaments that are of coral would be well; for this is—as it represents, as it is in itself of Creative Forces, or from the water itself. Red, white or coral in any form." (307-15)

When a twenty-nine-year-old woman asked whether or not colors made a difference and if so, what colors were best for her, the answer came: "Each body, each activity, each soul-entity vibrates better to this, that or the other color. As with this, certain colors of green and blue are those to which the body vibrates the better." (288-38) Demonstrating that color and vibration are somehow inextricably connected, Cayce once told a businessman that all vibration produces color. In other words, even vibrations that cannot be perceived by the human eye produce some type of color. (900-149)

The vibration of colors, especially as they manifest in flowers, were recommended to be a greater portion of the life's work for a forty-three-year-old gift shop manager. Cayce even suggested that because of this individual's affinity with the vibrations of flowers, it would be difficult for flowers to wilt in this woman's presence. The reading added:

> Music and flowers, then, should be the entity's work through this experience . . .
>
> For this entity has so oft been the music and the flower lady, until it becomes second nature to work in or with those either in arranging bouquets or corsages, or even the very foolish way of sending to those who have passed on. They need the flowers when they are here, not when they are in God's other room!
>
> In this manner, though, and in this work, may the entity not only minister to others, but it may do so in such a way and manner as for the beauty and the color, even the voice and tone of flowers to come to mean so much to people whom the entity would and could interest in such.   5122-1

During a follow-up reading in which the subjects of past lives and innate talents were explored for a thirty-two-year-old woman, Cayce provided a thorough discussion of vibration, music, harmony, and tone. To the question "What is the note of the musical scale to which I vibrate?" the answer came:

> As we have indicated, Ah–This is not R, but Ah–aum [A U M], see? These are the sounds. Those that respond to the centers of the body, in opening the centers so that the kundaline forces arise to that activity through those portions of the body. Sound these, and ye will find them in thyself. They are the manners or ways of seeking.
>
> For as ye have understood, if ye have read Him and His conversation with His friends, His disciples as respecting John–John was a great entity, none greater. And yet the least in the kingdom of heaven was greater than he. What meaneth this manner of speech?
>
> They that have wisdom are great, they that have under-standing as to the manner to *apply* same for the good of self *and* others–not for self at the expense of others, but for others–are in the awareness of the kingdom.
>
> Thus, as to the note of thy body–is there always the

response to just one? Yes. As we have indicated oft, for this entity as well as others, there are certain notes to which there is a response, but is it always the same? No more than thy moods or thy tendencies, *unless* ye have arisen to the understanding of perfect attunement.

When a violin or an instrument is attuned to harmony, is it out of tune when struck by the same motion, the same activity? Does it bring forth the same sound?

So with thy body, thy mind, thy soul. It is dependent upon the tuning—whether with the infinite or with self, or with worldly wisdom. For these, to be sure, become the mysteries of life to some—the mysteries of attuning. What seek ye? Him, self, or what?

He is within and beareth witness.

The tone, then—find it in thyself, if ye would be enlightened. To give the tune or tone as Do, Ah–aum–would mean little; unless there is the comprehending, the understanding of that to which ye are attempting to attune–in the spiritual, the mental, the material.

There *is* music in jazz, but is there perfect harmony in same?

There *is* harmony in a symphony, as in the voices as attuned to the infinite–a spirit and a body poured out in aid or the search for the soul.

There is no greater than that as may be expressed in that of, "O my son Absalom, my son, my son Absalom! would God I had died for thee, O Absalom, my son, my son!"

To what is this attuned? What *is* the note there?

That as of the realization of the lack of training the mind of the son in the way of the Lord, rather than in the knowledge of controlling individuals.

This, then, is indeed the way of harmony, the way of the pitch, the way of the tone. It is best sounded by what it arouses in thee–where, when, and under what circumstance.

We are through for the present.   2072-10

The vibratory quality of music was also recommended in the case of a thirty-one-year-old unemployed woman, who was encouraged to listen to classical music rather than jazz as a means of elevating her mood. She was also told that her mood was often affected by color; she was encouraged to stay away from *shades* of color and wear full tints instead. Her reading stated that in a former life she had been a member of the royal household under Queen Elizabeth I of England. For that reason it was suggested that the colors of royalty would especially appeal to her. Cayce also advised that the thing that would raise her vibration the most and essentially make her "invincible" to others was a small crown or coronet, such as that worn by the queen. However, Cayce's suggestion for her was to "wear it out of sight!" (2378-1)

Music was also recommended as a means of overcoming pessimism in the case of a fifty-two-year-old man challenged with frequent periods of depression. Told that music should always be a part of his life, the reading encouraged him:

> **And whenever there are the periods of depression, or the feeling low or forsaken, play music; especially stringed instruments of every nature. These will enable the entity to span that gulf as between pessimism and optimism.**
>
> **Keep optimistic as much as possible. Know that as ye give out ye receive, and that alone as ye have given away do ye possess.**   **1804-1**

In spite of the readings' assertion that vibrations have an ongoing impact upon people, on occasion Edgar Cayce advised individuals not to become overly focused upon the topic. Apparently, some individuals had an innate tendency to make the subject much more important in their lives than would be helpful for their own growth and development. For example, when a nineteen-year-old construction foreman received a Life reading, discussing his soul strengths and past lives, Cayce advised him not to place too great an emphasis on astrology and the vibrations of color and music. Evidently, in previous incarnations the young man had often delved into subjects that could be used for soothsaying and prophecy. Those incarnations included one as a Norseman, when he had become skilled in reading the signs of nature as well as the signs and movements of the creatures of the earth, and in ancient Persia when he had been a "soothsayer" and a "seer."

Because of these experiences, the young man had developed a tendency to make astrology, the study of vibrations, and tools such as these ends unto themselves, rather than what Cayce would call "signs along the way." It was for this reason that the reading advised the individual that nothing surpassed the power of his own will. Cayce encouraged him not to let this type of information become the focus it had been for him previously. When the young man asked about his vibrational colors, the reading responded: "As indicated, *well* that such as these be forgotten in the experiences of the entity. For there are the inclinations to let same become the motivative force rather than the *spirituality of* an influence!" (1450-1)

However, when the same individual asked, "To what musical notes do I vibrate?" the following response came: "The entity *may* vibrate to the higher spheres, if the purposes, the inclinations, the tendencies are set in that direction. *Listen* to the notes of the combinations of F and G." Nevertheless, a final warning came when the question was asked: "What are my lucky numbers?" The answer was: "From one to as high as you can count, if you will apply them in your experience! As has been indicated, do not let these become the stumblingstones thou hast heretofore."

For the most part, the Cayce information discusses the influence of vibration in terms of its helpfulness in the lives of most individuals. For example, a woman with a talent for both interior decorating and music was encouraged to use music in her work with decorating. When she asked how that could be accomplished, Cayce stated that the vibration of music actually enabled her to tune into her clients and would help her create harmony in the homes where she was working. (2881-3)

On another occasion, a Life reading exploring the positive, innate influences regarding the subject of vibrations was given to a fourteen-year-old girl seeking guidance and career advice. In her case, the vibrational qualities of colors, the elements, and jewelry had all been important influences in her previous incarnations and could serve her just as well in the present. In fact, Cayce stated that she had previously been a prophetess and seer in Egypt and had used her psychic talents to be extremely helpful to others—a gift and a motivation that remained with her. During the early portion of the foundations of the American colonies, the young woman had also been supportive of those individuals who had been falsely accused of witchcraft—an act that had caused her to be "ducked" into water. At the time, she innately understood how psychic experiences manifest as well as how individuals often pick up psychic information from the emotions and vibrations of others.

In an earlier lifetime, she had been a Greek musician who had used the harmonies and vibrations of color and music to bring physical and mental health to others. In a number of her lifetimes, she had been of great aid to many people. Throughout these incarnations she had also become extremely psychic and sensitive—a gift, the readings advised her, which was not always easy to deal with: "For the entity is not only able and capable to receive the vibrations of individuals about the entity as to their colors but as to their vibrations. And these then make for a sensitiveness that is often disturbing to the entity." However, the encouragement came, "To thine own self be true and thou wilt not be false to anyone."

The girl was told that her own vibrations were extremely powerful and radiated from her so that she often had an effect upon others: "Hence many, many, *many* are influenced by the entity . . ." In terms of advice in working with her own sensitivity to vibrations, Cayce recommended the following:

> **Know that when there is felt, seen or experienced those vibrations of low, leaden or dark reds, these are as dangers . . .**
> **Then study those influences. And know when such arise in the experience that warnings are ahead, and govern the associations and the activities accordingly.**
> **When there is felt that glow of orange, and the violet hues with the orange, know that these bespeak of sentimentality in the experience and are not always good; yet these in their proper relationships should be a portion of the experiences that make for a joy and an understanding; and it is indeed in such experiences–in which one may know what such vibrations and such colors mean–that the individuals may be trusted.**
> **When these reach those stages as to where there is felt the lighter red, and those that turn to shades of green with**

the influences that make for shadings into white, then these trust, these hold to; for such individuals, such associations, may bring in the experience of the entity that which will make for spiritual enlightenment, a mental understanding, and the influences that would bring helpful influences in every experience.

Hence the opal that is called the change, with the moonstone, should be stones about the body or entity oft. Wear the fire opal as a locket about the neck. This would be well. Not upon the hands nor upon the wrists, but about the neck.

Wear the others, as of the pearl with moonstone or the like, as rings or amulets or anklets; but never those upon the neck or in the ears–rather upon the extremities; for they will make for the bringing out–in the experiences of those the entity meets–of those very colors and vibrations that have been indicated to which the entity is so sensitive.   **1406-1**

A twenty–one–year–old woman whose entire family had been enthusiasts of the Edgar Cayce information was told that her work with music, attunement, healing, and the raising of consciousness and vibrations from an earlier incarnation in one of the Egyptian temples remained a part of her being in the present. Perhaps because of her intense focus on these topics in a previous lifetime, the readings suggested that she could work with both visualization and musical tones to raise her consciousness to be more in keeping with the Christ Consciousness within. This ability was apparently more pronounced in her than in others, as she was told, ". . . few there be in the earth in the present that may attain to a concentrated or a continued association in the spiritual forces of their activity, as this soul!" (275-37)

A professional harpist by training, Miss (275) asked why the higher notes in music seemed to move her emotionally whereas the lower ones did not. The answer came that it was in response to her own attunement and how she resonated to the vibrational tone of the notes themselves:

That the attunement of the body is of the highest is indicated by this very experience. That the sensitiveness of the body in its high mental and spiritual abilities is attuned to the higher influences is seen by these experiences. As this then may be said of many conditions that are accredited to influences in the manifested form of a material world. Not that the body-mind or the spiritual forces are influenced *by* the notes, but that the vibrations and the *attunement* of the impulse or the soul forces *is* at the high pitch is attested by the effect of this attunement–and the effect upon the body, see?   275-37

Four years later, during the course of another reading given to the same person, Miss (275) asked about the advisability of following up on electrical treatments that had been recommended to her by a doctor, in order to help her with nerve damage in one of her teeth. Cayce advised instead that she have the modern–day equivalent of a root canal or that she consider healing the nerve damage with meditation, breathing exercises, attunement, and a chant she had used previously. He also stated that this approach would not work for everyone with this type of problem, but it would work for her:

. . . as we find it can be accomplished much more satisfactorily within self by the right character of meditation and breathing exercise–which would be those with the body seated *in* what is ordinarily termed as Chinese or Japanese fashion, and with the chant that has been a portion of the body–of the Ar-ar-r-r---e-e-e---o-o-o--m-m-m, in the deep breathing and the circular motions of the body, and the carrying of the directing of the spiritual influences and the mental activity to the glandular forces of the body; raising these *within* self, and directing them to that to be accomplished would be the manner.

Not that this becomes as an Egyptian or an East Indian chant, but keeping the mental attitude of the Christ-Consciousness within that is purifying, is magnifying the abilities for peace, quiet, yet *attuning* self to the aliveness of not only the emotions but to the mental application for *constructive* experiences in the body and mind.

These are much better than depending upon either suggestion from without or the application of any form of

electrical or mechanical appliance for the raising of the vibrations for *this* body, [275].
This would not do for *all*, but can be accomplished within self.   275-45

Parents of an eleven-month-old boy were told that their son had once been a healer in a temple in Atlantis and, at the time, had used chants and music as a means of attuning individuals to higher vibrations, facilitating healing in the process. Cayce suggested that this innate talent, as well as other past lives that had been devoted to music, would enable the child to play any instrument and be extremely gifted in music and voice. The readings stated that he also had an ear for harmony and should be frequently exposed to the music of symphonies during his upbringing as a means of reawakening his musical talents. (2584-1)

As is reflected in a number of the case histories mentioned above, oftentimes individuals who received Cayce readings were told that healing is the desired outcome for using the vibrations of sound and/or color. The following instances provide further examples from the Cayce archives.

Parents of a teenage girl suffering from speech and hearing problems (including secretions and inflammation in her eustachian tube) were told to encourage their daughter to begin working with the vibrations of music and color in addition to other therapies. Cayce recommended enabling the girl to "feel the vibrations in stringed musical instruments," such as the violin and the guitar. He also recommended that the girl frequently wear clothing that contained "deep violet and *red* red." The reading suggested that the vibrations of the color and the music would facilitate healing in both speech and hearing, so much so that the parents would quickly be able to see the results for themselves. (4223-3)

Another woman, who was essentially blind and could only see some variations in light and shade, was encouraged to study music. Cayce stated that her essential problem was a paralysis of the optic nerve, which could be reversed. Apparently, the vibration of music could help to facilitate that healing process. (4531-2)

On another occasion, a twenty-year-old musician was told that he had the innate talent to help heal through color, vibration, and tone. It was suggested that the vibration of his music had the effect of bringing harmony to those individuals who were troubled with anxiety and pressure from the outside world. The reading also stated that his music was helpful to any individual who had become ill and had taken on a vibration of illness within her or his own body. (824-1)

Similarly, a forty-three-year-old woman was told that her greatest contribution toward others would be through making healing music and sharing the vibration of that music with others:

> **For, whether it is in a service in the home or elsewhere, it can be done in the nature of harmony in a musical vibration; whether it is in the ministering to the needs of others, as of interesting others, or as an aid or helpfulness to smaller groups, or children, or adults, through harmony, through music; for through the application of self in those directions there may come, there may be found, the greater abilities not only to hold to that already gained but to add to self the abilities of others in such, in being a contributory cause to a helpful influence or force in the minds of others.   5201-1**

Rather than using music for others, a forty-seven-year-old housewife was told that her singing voice helped raise her own vibrations, making a closer attunement with the divine possible. Cayce told the woman that it was music alone that could span the bridge between the finite mind and the infinite of the divine, and that her music and chanting ("Ar-ar-r-r----e-e-e----ooo---mmm") could bring to her an awareness of His all-abiding presence. (1158-10)

Chanting was also encouraged for a thirty-year-old model. Her reading stated that like all individuals, ultimately, she had been seeking her relationship to the divine. In her case, it was suggested that this relationship could be discovered by attuning to the chant "*home*"— "O-h-m-mmmmm":

> **For, as has been indicated from the innate experience as well as from the longings within, a home–*home*–with all its deeper, inner meanings, is a portion of the entity's desire; to**

know, to experience, to have the "feel" of, to have the surroundings of that implied by the word *home*! Is it any wonder then that in all of thy meditation, Ohm–O-h-m-mmmmm has ever been, is ever a portion of that which raises self to the highest influence and the highest vibrations throughout its whole being that may be experienced by the entity?   1286-1

A past-life talent as a healer working with color, vibration, and the laying on of hands apparently resurfaced with a forty-seven-year-old woman who was encouraged to again apply herself as a healer in the present. The color blue-green was also recommended to be a portion of the woman's attire for its healing vibration, and the woman was told that her own high vibration was often soothing to others:

For the vibrations are high, and these are of the healing nature to those especially who are troubled with those things that have raised the emotions to detrimental influences to the whole of the assimilation; the assimilating system, to the nervous system, to the heart's activity, to the influences where destruction of self is at times felt necessary.
    The entity may soothe, the entity may cause all such to become quiet.   1469-7

Similarly, working with healing was recommended to a thirty-six-year-old schoolteacher who was encouraged to use vibrations, as they manifested in color, tone, and spiritual healing. Her reading suggested that she follow the example of Jesus, finding whatever means of vibratory healing would be helpful to those individuals she encountered:

For, as has so oft been given, and as demonstrated in the experience of the Great Physician [Jesus], He met the needs of the individual–whether by the spoken word, vibration, or application of means that attune–the dissenting tissue or body to the divinity that is in each soul, each body who has acknowledged, who lives in the Christ Consciousness.
                                                              2441-4

Shortly thereafter, the woman wrote Edgar Cayce to thank him for the reading, which she said had been extremely helpful to her. She also asked for additional information on healing and vibration, to which Edgar Cayce wrote back and responded in part:

> **If I understand aright . . . the vibration of your body [is] so high that when you lay your hands on some one else the healing influence passes to them–that is a poor explanation but hope you get what I am trying to say. That as I understand is why–or how you feel the vibration of the spoken word–and how color to you is felt as vibrations. Of course color is vibration–but do very few feel it as vibration. Yes am sure you can attune yourself so, that you can know the real need of those who merely speak to you–and best of all you will be able to help them by tuning them to their needs physically and mentally. Oh yes, carries a great obligation with it–for if the blind lead the blind, both will fall in the ditch, but you have the attunement and the will and may be the shining light for many.**

In addition to the topic of vibrations as they relate to both color and sound, oftentimes the Cayce information discussed the important vibrational qualities of specific stones and jewelry. For example, on a number of occasions the readings stated that the vibration of lapis lazuli was actually helpful in terms of manifesting psychic abilities. In the case of a fifty–seven–year–old man, lapis lazuli was recommended, as it helped to "make for the raising of the attunement in self through meditation." During the course of this reading, the individual was encouraged to work with the vibrations of various stones in his work with meditation and personal attunement.

For the same person, the reading stated that agate and beryl helped to create a vibration that facilitated an awakening of "receptiveness" within the man's inner self. He was encouraged to keep various kinds of stones about himself and to see them as manifestations of the creative force, not somehow mystical within themselves. He was also told that the vibrations of astronomy, numerology, metals, and stones had all had their influence upon him as a healer throughout a variety of his earthly experiences.

For example, in a previous experience as a Talladega Indian, he had served his people as a medicine man. From that lifetime, he had brought forth a number of traits and talents, including the ability to enter into a very deep state of meditation. During an incarnation at the time of the early Church, he had acquired the ability to preach and to teach. From a lifetime as a desert nomad, he had gained the knowledge and ability to do laying-on-of-hands spiritual healing—a gift that remained with him in the present. In summing up his talents in the present, Cayce had the following to say: "The abilities to heal, the abilities to teach, the abilities to minister, all are thine!" (707-1)

Lapis lazuli was also recommended as a vibrational conduit for manifesting psychic abilities, during a reading given to a twenty-three-year-old electrical engineer who was a resident of New York City. Cayce recommended that the individual wear lapis as a pendant, either on his waist or wrist. He also encouraged the young man to try an experiment just to prove to himself whether or not the vibrational quality of the stone actually worked:

This may be—will be—a very interesting experiment for the body. Go to the New York Museum of Natural History. Sit by a large quantity of this type of stone and listen at it sing! Do it in the open! Don't let others make a fool of you, or their remarks overcome you—but sit by it and listen at it sing; for it does!   **440-3**

Six months later, the same individual asked for follow-up information on how the stones worked to help facilitate psychic receptivity. Essentially, Cayce stated that the stones were most effective with individuals who already had a vibrational affinity for, or who were in vibrational accord with, the energy put off by the lapis lazuli. That affinity, in effect, helped the individual's own psychic sensitivity "step up" to the next level, enabling the individual to be even more psychic than was normally the case. (440-18)

A twenty-eight-year-old actress was advised that "the stone to which this entity vibrates" was a bloodstone. She was encouraged to wear a bloodstone, cut in the shape of a triangle with oval edges, as a means of creating a vibration that would help her become more successful in life. The reading continued: "This about the body brings that vibration which will be beneficial; not merely as a 'good luck' charm, not merely as something upon which to depend, but as an influence, a vibration about the entity." (2163-1)

When a twenty-two-year-old student asked for career guidance during the course of her Life reading, Cayce recommended that she draw upon her innate skills as an artist. The reading also encouraged her to wear pearls as a means of elevating her mood. Cayce counseled that since the pearl was produced by irritation, the vibrations of pearls actually enabled most wearers to build a resistance to becoming easily irritated. Her greatest skills seemed to be in art—especially art that used various precious stones in its creation. Her reading suggested that she could also awaken artistic talent in people, bringing the vibrations of harmony and joy into the lives of others. When she asked how she might more fully develop her own creative talents, the reading advised:

Anything that pertains to art and art's expression. Those things particularly in those very associations of stones and their vibrations may be as a portion of self; knowing the vibrations, the *effect* of vibrations of stones and their wearing of same upon the bodies of others. This will not only be interesting, but will make for abilities within self to know others.   **1189-1**

Wearing a pearl was also recommended in the case of a man prone to an explosive temper. As Cayce described him, "For the entity can get mad, and when it is mad it is really *mad!*" (2533-1) The individual was told that having a pearl (such as in his pocket or on a ring) would create a vibration that would help him have a more even temperament.

Another woman who apparently needed some constructive energy in her thought processes and life was encouraged to work with pearl and moonstone. The reading explained their influence: "Not that they influence, but create by their *vibration* an element through which the *mental* and the spiritual forces of the entity may vibrate for constructive experience in their activity." Cayce also recommended that the woman consider being around flowers in her meditations (especially the pansy), as they helped to reproduce the "vibrations from the earth" and would enable her to remain centered during her meditations. (1037-1)

A secretary was also encouraged to wear moonstone close to her body, such as moonstone hanging from a chain that she could wear around her neck. The reading stated that the stone would provide her with a helpful vibration, giving her strength. Cayce went on to suggest that previously, in her most recent past life, she had used the same kind of stone in Arkansas, when she had found moonstone to be a source of comfort and personal fortitude. (5125-1)

On one occasion, a receptionist asked about the advisability of wearing an antique pearl necklace that had been given to her and whether or not the pearls carried a healing vibration. Her reading stated that eventually the pearls would pick up the vibrations of the woman's own "body-forces," at which time they would be helpful, but at the present they contained the vibrations of the previous owner, which were not necessarily helpful. In order to expedite the pearls being more appropriate for her own vibrations, Cayce suggested that they be "demagnetized" through the use of an ultra-violet ray for one-tenth of a second: "This will demagnetize it and set it for better body vibration for this body." (951-6)

On another occasion, a woman suffering from depression, nervousness, and headaches was encouraged not to wear any jewelry at all during her healing process. Apparently, the vibrations that she was attempting to change within her body would be absorbed into the jewelry and inadvertently create an energy pattern that would make overcoming the problem even more difficult. Instead, she was advised to engage in activities that involved others and then, once she was well on the way to recovery, only to wear very, very old jewelry, as it would apparently serve as some type of grounding vibration for her. (1540-3)

In order to assist her attunement during meditation, a sixty-year-old doctor was advised to have chrysolite or amethyst near her during her meditations. She was also told that the color purple would help her attunement, as would the odor of lavender. (688-2)

In 1943 Cayce's biography *There is a River*, coupled with the article "Miracle Man of Virginia Beach" in *Coronet* magazine, led to all kinds of publicity for Edgar Cayce. Rather than only giving two readings a day, as had been advised by his own readings, Cayce began giving many, many more and having his secretary schedule them way in advance, just as a means of attempting to catch up with the requests for help. It was this type of demand that Cayce was facing when a fifty-year-old woman wrote for help, after reading his biography. Because of her questions and the number of times she asked the same thing in a variety of ways, it became very clear that fear had been an ongoing motivational influence in her life.

The woman's first request for a reading came on November 15, 1943. In that letter, she asked quite a number of questions about marriage— whether she would ever be married, where she could find the proper husband, and whether she would have material success that might come on account of a marriage. A legal assistant, she also asked for career advice. Eight days later, she sent a follow-up request for a reading, reiterating many of the same questions. Within a week of the second letter, she sent a third request. Because of Edgar Cayce's full schedule, she was told that her reading could not be scheduled until early in 1944, but she sent a fourth request in February 1944 anyway, restating the same questions and others. Her fifth request was mailed on March 7, 1944, in which she again summarized her need for help:

> . . . **There are one or two questions I have been asking, searching for the answer for 10 years . . . I DO NEED A LIFE READING. A reading that will tell me about marriage . . . I WANT MARRIAGE AND MY OWN HOME. HOW CAN I SECURE THIS PERFECT MARRIAGE AND PERFECT HOME? There is a man E. D. T., whom I knew over 10 years ago in . . . , who flies his plane, or somebody's airplane, over me, 3 times a day and more, over my office, my home or wherever I am, even in church. I want this man to know I love him. Am I supposed to marry him, in spite of the fact that I am older than he? I would like to get a letter to him. Shall I do this? And if so, where can I locate him? I have tried the airports near here, but my letter came back to me.**

Am I supposed to take care of father? Shall I buy a house? Where? . . .

Nine days later, after someone in the Cayce office apparently wrote her and asked her to remain patient, her sixth letter was mailed with the following statement: "I, of course, realize that the person in your office who thought I do not want to wait my turn is mistaken. If I seemed impatient, you must consider that a great compliment . . . Who would not be impatient under those circumstances? . . ." Her seventh letter with "revised questions" was mailed on April 5. Finally, her reading took place on April 16, 1944.

Cayce began the reading by assuring the woman that she had many talents but that she was often beset with fears and insecurities: ". . . we find an entity well gifted in many things, yet subject to much of that which is interpreted in self as fear." (5030-1) The reading went on to advise: ". . . be warned regarding fear, its sources, and as to how to eliminate same." Cayce suggested that in addition to fear, the woman was oftentimes jealous of what others appeared to have, what she felt like she lacked. The woman's personal anxieties had also brought her to the point in which she was even fearful of certain days of the month.

In order to address the woman's various fears and insecurities, the reading recommended setting spiritual ideals and applying the fruits of the spirit: "Remember through faith, love, kindness, patience, longsuffering, one may cast out fear." In addition, she was encouraged to use the vibrations of any kind of green stone to help her work through her fears. Cayce assured her that such vibrations "may keep the entity from fear." Shortly after receiving the reading, the woman expressed her thanks:

> **Your reading for me was wonderful, indeed, even tho it made me cry . . . Apparently, in this life, I must overcome FEAR, as it relates to men and marriage, and to all other things, too. WELL, I will pray, pray, very, very hard, and trust only in God, and stop worrying and fearing . . .**

On another occasion, a fifty-eight-year-old jeweler seeking help from the readings was told that the vibrations of precious stones had also been of interest to him during a past life in Egypt. Then, as now, he had often worked with gold, rubies, diamonds, and emeralds and had found that each stone possessed a different "spirit," or vibration. Diamonds seemed to vibrate with personal peace or selfishness, depending on the wearer. Pearls could create irritation or facilitate peace, depending on the wearer as well. Cayce suggested that in the present the jeweler would find that all stones possess a unique vibration and that the vibration could have a positive or a negative influence upon an individual, depending upon how it interacted with the wearer's own vibration. (3657-1) Another person was told that opals, for some people, could be associated with the vibration of fickleness. (2522-1)

When a forty-year-old man complained of feeling powerless in terms of achieving success in his life, Cayce recommended that he consider wearing a ruby ring or having a ruby stone upon his body. Rather than having the individual believe that the ruby possessed power within itself, Cayce suggested instead that the vibration of the ruby would help his own powers of concentration. The reading went on to say,

Each element, each stone, each variation of stone, has its own atomic movement, held together by the units of energy that in the universe are concentrated in that particular activity. Hence they come under varied activities according to their color, vibration or emanation.

In this particular one (the ruby) there is that fitness with that which has been the experience of *this* soul, this entity, through material expression. Hence it is an aid, a crutch to lean upon. But, as has always been given, let it be a stepping-stone; *not* that which thou *standest* only upon! 531-3

Taken together, the Edgar Cayce information on the vibrations of sound, color, and stone suggests that for many people, each of these has the potential to be a helpful influence in a variety of ways. Some individuals may find that they possess an affinity with certain vibrations, and that affinity resonates with something deep within. Others may turn to vibrations as a grounding or even a protective influence. Certainly, vibrations have a connection to the human body, the spiritual centers, and even personal attunement. On other occasions, the energy associated with vibrations might be helpful in stimulating certain emotions, motivations, or even response patterns. Regardless of how they may be used, however, the important thing is to realize that all vibrations are simply variations of the one force in motion—they are aspects *of* the one force and not the force within themselves. In fact, the true rationale for any use of vibration may be summed up in Cayce's answer to an individual who received a series of insights on the power of vibration when she asked, "What is the main purpose of this incarnation?" The response came, "To glorify the Christ-Consciousness in the earth—in the lives of those with whom ye come in contact, and to live the same thyself." (2441-4)

VIBRATIONS
Vibrations and Cayce's "Appliances"

Yes, we have the appliance here. This, as we see, is a form of that as has been given for the vibrations of the body and as beneficial to the human organism in producing an equalization of the vibrations necessary to produce the equalization of the system.   *1800-6*

BECAUSE EVERYTHING IS VIBRATION, on many occasions, the Edgar Cayce readings recommended using the ways in which vibrations operate as a means of stimulating healing and facilitating such things as the expansion of consciousness or even helping humankind in general. In fact, these three purposes—physical healing, the expansion of consciousness, and providing various ways to assist humankind—are all at the heart of more than two thousand readings that were given on the use and creation of what has been called Cayce's "appliances."[4]

---

[4] Additional information on the Edgar Cayce appliances, their uses, and where they can be purchased can be found at EdgarCayce.org.

Each of these appliances is essentially a device that utilizes vibrations in a variety of ways. In terms of healing, the readings recommended several devices that reportedly use gentle electrotherapy as a means of facilitating the body's own healing vibrations. In terms of other uses for mechanisms that utilized vibrations, Cayce described a number of appliances for such things as perceiving higher states of consciousness, creating a perpetual motion machine, and eliminating radio static. What may be most exciting about this component of the Cayce information is that it often explores a variety of potentials for vibrations that have essentially been overlooked by the modern world.

As discussed previously, the Edgar Cayce material states that each organ and function of the body creates a vibration all its own. When that ideal vibration is adversely affected in any way, disease and illness become the result. In order to stimulate the proper vibrations within an individual and promote healing, on many occasions a variety of appliances was recommended as a means of using a tiny electrical charge and/or a vibrational current to help balance or rejuvenate the body's own vibratory functions. Two appliances that were specifically created and recommended by the readings are the Radio–Active Appliance and the Wet Cell Battery. On other occasions, other appliances were also recommended because of the way in which they used vibration to promote healing. These appliances were not necessarily unique to the readings. Perhaps the most frequently mentioned appliance of this type was the Violet Ray, which was recommended for a variety of conditions. Each of these will be discussed in greater detail in the context of case histories from the Cayce files.

Radio-Active Appliance (Radial Appliance), or Impedance Device

Known by several names and used for a variety of conditions, Edgar Cayce stated that the Radial Appliance utilizes the body's own electrical current, or life force, to coordinate balance and homeostasis at the vibrational level, facilitating healing in the process. Named the Radio–Active appliance, before the days of atomic energy, the appliance is not radioactive, nor does it generate any energy within itself. In order to avoid confusion, it is now generally known as the Radial Appliance. From the readings' perspective, this device is "beneficial to the human organism in producing an equalization of the vibrations necessary to produce the equalization of the system." (1800–6) As early as 1925, the readings suggested that this appliance had commercial value, and a number of readings were obtained to give specific instructions for the creation and use of the Radial Appliance.

In 1933 Gray Salter, then supervisor of the "appliance department," wrote an article that briefly described the workings of vibrations within the physical body and how the Radial Appliance worked to equalize the vibratory rate of the body. The following is an excerpt from that article:

> Let us compare the nervous systems to telegraph systems, with the brain as the central receiving and sending station. Within a human body there is the central nervous system, consisting of the brain and the spinal cord; and the peripheral system, consisting of the cerebrospinal and sympathetic nerve fibers. The brain sends and receives messages along the large spinal cord which in turn is connected at various plexuses or stations with the nerves of the cerebrospinal and sympathetic which pass to all parts of the body, forming a complete network of tiny nerve fibres. Along the various branches of this network vibrations pass with lightning rapidity to and from the various sub-stations and the central station, the brain. In the telegraph system, a weak place or break in the wires will cause a short-circuit. Transformers or boosters are used to boost up messages over long distances. In the body, a strain or binding will cause incoordination. Impulses, as messages, will not reach the different parts of the body properly. The circulation is thus affected and inflammation results.
>
> All matter, whether organic or inorganic, has a period of vibration or frequency. When this is changed, the entire structure changes and a reaction takes place. For example, water may be heated until it is reduced to steam. The vibratory rate or period of frequency has been altered. Every particle of matter has its peculiar vibratory rate . . .

The value of this appliance lies in its equalization of the *existing* vibratory rate of the body. As we have already noted, strain of any kind will produce incoordination at various centers of the connecting nervous systems. By passing the natural current from the body through this equalizer, opportunity is given for the rebuilding of the part affected.
1800-17 Reports

From Cayce's perspective, the Radial Appliance has a beneficial effect on a variety of health issues—rheumatoid arthritis, insomnia, migraines, colds and congestion, menopause, depression, obesity, Alzheimer's, and anemia, just to name a few. One of the case histories from the Cayce files in which the Radial Appliance was recommended was for a fifty-three-year-old philosophy professor with hypertension. A reading attributed the hypertension to an overall problem with the body's assimilation, circulation, respiration, and elimination processes (957-2). Although each of these systems was working in cooperation and coordination one with another, none was operating normally; instead, the systems had found a way to function in disharmony together.

In order to eliminate the hypertension, a regimen of therapies was recommended that included a change of diet, osteopathic adjustments, and improved eliminations. However, the individual was told that the most beneficial aspect of treatment would be raising his vibrations through the use of the Radial Appliance. Cayce told the professor that although the Radial Appliance appeared small and of little value, its effect would help to normalize his body's systems, effectively curing his problem:

While they are seemingly of little or no use from outward appearance, their constructive forces are in an *orderly* manner, and in keeping with those laws that replenish through continuity of vibratory rates built or created in various portions of the system, and equalized through that vibration sent out. This enables the quieting, then, from within, and allows the forces to become predominant that are constructive to *vitality* in system.   **957-3**

The Radial Appliance was also an important part of the healing regimen recommended to a fifty–nine–year–old nurse with a variety of problems including arthritis, anxiety, depression, and neurasthenia (an early twentieth–century diagnosis that appears to have a close connection to the contemporary chronic fatigue syndrome). Cayce suggested that many of her problems were connected to an incoordination of the proper vibrations associated with homeostasis, and for that reason the Radial Appliance would be extremely beneficial to her. During the course of the reading, the woman asked if the appliance would help "correct short hours of sleep and many other troubles." To which Cayce replied that the appliance would help produce a "correct equilibrium in system," having a beneficial effect on her vibrations and her nervous system. (4329-2)

Another individual with arthritis was encouraged to use the Radial Appliance and meditation in his treatment program. The arthritis had progressed to the point where it was severely impacting the man's mobility, although he was only thirty–seven years old at the time of the reading. Cayce stated that in addition to the appliance, the individual's attitude would play an extremely important role in the healing process. With this in mind, the man was encouraged to meditate on the following thoughts, stating them in his own words if he desired:

> *Our Father who art in heaven, hallowed be thy name! May the love, O God, thou has shown to the sons of men, be manifested in me and my body in such measures that I may show forth to my fellow men thy love as is manifested through the gift of thy Son to those who have lost their way. May my body, my mind, be used in a service to thee, through the kindnesses, the gentlenesses, those hopes that may be brought to my fellow men by and through the efforts of my body, my mind, my activities; that all the glory may be to thee. In his name we seek, O God!*

Cayce's rationale was then given:

> **This would be the manner then of the attitude, that the will of the Father may be done. For he knoweth what each hath need of, even before we ask; but by the attuning of the**

vital forces of the body by those energizing experiences of the metals in the Radio-Active [Radial] appliance we attune the Infinite within self to the Infinite without. Then the words of the meditation and prayer create that vibration, the emotions so that the influences that may be applied externally, internally, through the diet, through all portions of the activities, may bring coordination, cooperation in the physical forces of the body.   1211-2

The appliance was also recommended to a forty-five-year-old woman with a cold and congestion. She happened to be underweight and complained of feeling tired. Cayce stated that the exhaustion was due to the incoordination of the vibrations in her body. In her case, the appliance would prove beneficial as an equalizer for circulation and vibrations, and for relieving congestion. In the language of the readings:

This, as we see, has this effect in the system: Equalizing of circulation to its normal condition, forcing coordination by the nerve reaction in system and relieving congestion in any portion of body same may occur at that time, bringing the better normal sleep to body, giving the physical forces the opportunity for recuperation through the equalized circulation.   538-12

The suggestions for using the Radial Appliance were followed, and the woman apparently returned to normal health much quicker than had been anticipated. In fact, a few months later, the woman's husband made the following report: ". . . I am sure the Appliance has done [538] a wonderful lot of good . . . she weighs a hundred, about the first time she's ever reached that weight. She's looking mighty well . . ."

One individual was told that a lack of circulation in his eustachian tubes was attributing to his hearing loss and that by using the Radial Appliance, a more "correct" vibration for his body would be created, improving the circulation and eventually resulting in improved hearing (2220-1). On another occasion, a fifty-eight-year-old minister with a variety of health problems was told that his painful abdominal hernia could be assisted without surgery through the use of the Radial

Appliance. When the individual asked whether the abdominal tissue could actually be healed, the reading replied that the balanced vibration generated through the use of the appliance would promote healing: "That's why the *low* electrical forces are given . . . so that the activities of the blood supply, through low electrical forces, will produce better coagulation. See, there is a lack in the blood supply of those of the gluten that make for better or proper coagulation . . ." (1466-2)

In 1930 a forty-five-year-old man with insomnia was told that his problem was the result of an incoordination between his mental and physical bodies. For that reason the Radial Appliance was recommended as a means to help balance and equalize the mind and body. In fact, Cayce stated that simply by connecting him to the appliance, "he will sleep." (45-5) A fifty-six-year-old woman with severe migraine headaches was encouraged to obtain spinal adjustments, to eat a more balanced diet, to cultivate a more spiritual attitude, and to use the Radial Appliance in order to overcome her headaches. (3169-1) The appliance was also recommended as a means of equalizing the body for a forty-seven-year-old woman who was experiencing menopause. (1133-1)

Another female patient, with severe allergy problems, including allergies to the sun and to physical exertion, was told that her condition was principally a problem of improper vibrations: "In this particular body we find the glands are so affected, by the variation in the various forms of vibration as may be created in system, that by light, by association, by physical exertion . . . may produce the condition . . ." (5578-1) Her reading suggested a number of therapies designed to stimulate and equalize normal vibrations, including osteopathy and the Radial Appliance. Emphasizing the impact of vibrations on her overall condition, the reading asserted, "We must change the vibrations if we would have the *permanent* relief for the body."

To be sure, the efficacy of Cayce's recommendations could only be as helpful as the individuals' willingness to use them. For example, in 1944 a forty-eight-year-old railroad employee was diagnosed with progressive multiple sclerosis. Cayce recommended using the Radial Appliance in order to stop the degeneration of his muscles. Use of the appliance was started, and a doctor's notation on file suggests that the effect was measurable: "Mr. [5158] has shown considerable improvement, and is now able to walk and has regained somewhat the use of his bowels and controls his bladder. He has renewed confidence and courage, and is thrilling his family with his optimism." (5158-1 Reports) However, a follow-up notation from the doctor stated that eventually the patient stopped using the appliance. When the appliance was discontinued, all of the recovery that the patient had made stopped. The disease progressed and the patient was dead within five years.

Another lack of follow-through occurred after a 1944 reading for a young woman. She had written Edgar Cayce requesting help, and included the following background information: "When I was 9 years old I had Infantile Paralysis. My right leg is paralyzed, and I walk with a brace and cane. I do get around extremely well and people think I have merely broken an ankle . . ." A reading was obtained in which Edgar Cayce recommended a change in diet, working with spiritual ideals, massage, and the use of the Radial Appliance. Although a follow-up reading was not requested, Cayce hinted at the fact that the problem was due to a prior incarnation, suggesting that the young woman's illness was simply the result of karmic memory: ". . . the entity in the limbs has been meeting its own self from other experiences." In terms of the appliance, the reading had this to say:

> **Do use the Radio-Active [Radial] Appliance as an equalizer. Attach to the right wrist, left ankle, left wrist, right ankle; these circulated about the body. Attach the same plate first each time to the body. Be sure no other body uses the Appliance. There is no vibration until you have attuned yourself to same, as may be felt from same. But use this an hour each day and use this as a period for meditation, for attuning thyself to the divine which is within.   5326-1**

In spite of the fact that the individual had originally written "I have found a doctor who is willing and confident in doing something with my lameness" . . . and that "he is very interested in your work and would be willing to cooperate with whatever information could be revealed through you . . . "—no report on the woman's condition was ever received until 1973, when Cayce's secretary added the following to the report file: "A young man told me today that he met [5326] in the D.C. area; she has a good Gov. job and seems well adjusted to her physical disability. She told him she did not follow the reading, since she didn't understand the Radio-Active [Radial] Appliance nor where to obtain it." Obviously, no results could be obtained from a treatment regimen that was not followed.

Since the Radial Appliance uses the body's own energy to equalize the system, maintaining the proper, constructive thoughts are an extremely important aspect of utilizing the appliance. In fact, if the individual has a negative or pessimistic outlook while using the appliance, the appliance will only redistribute that negativity throughout the whole system. In addition to the use of meditation and spiritual ideals, Cayce often suggested certain inspirational passages from the Bible, particularly the 30th chapter of Deuteronomy and the 14th, 15th, 16th, and 17th chapters of John. In addition, in the same way as the readings state that jewelry picks up and absorbs the vibration of the wearer, individuals were cautioned not to share their Radial Appliance with anyone else. The readings also cautioned against using any form of electrotherapy while alcohol is in the system. Don't use the appliance if you have been drinking!

Over the years, the readings' recommendations for the Radial Appliance had become so frequent that by 1940, Cayce's son Hugh Lynn wrote an expanded article on the use of the appliances, which was mailed to all individuals who received readings recommending either the Radial Appliance or Wet Cell Appliance. An excerpted version of that article follows.

THE RADIO-ACTIVE [henceforth "Radial"] APPLIANCE
—by Hugh Lynn Cayce

HISTORY: The Radial Appliance was first described in individual psychic readings given by Edgar Cayce over twenty years ago. The crude form of the first Appliance has been greatly improved through the years. Research work on this Appliance was done in 1928, 1929, and 1930 in the Cayce Hospital at Virginia Beach, Virginia. Under the direction of physicians and technicians excellent test conditions were set

up and valuable reports secured . . .

CONSTRUCTION AND OPERATION: The Appliance is made up of two insulated steel bars packed in charcoal in a metal container. Flexible wire leads are attached to each bar and are connected to the body by means of small silver plates. The Appliance is placed in a small jar of cracked ice and allowed to remain for fifteen minutes before being used.

The Radial Appliance directly affects the circulation. The vibratory current of the body passes through it, the temperature of the Appliance being lower than that of the body, building up a low impulse which is given off through the anodes attached to the extremities of the body. The construction of this Appliance makes it possible for the impulses to be regular and even. It is thus effective without the tensing of nerves and muscles, which is frequently the case where high frequency currents are used. The Appliance is not connected with any electric current and causes no discomfort to the body while treatments are being taken, producing rest and relaxation instead.

WHEN TO BE USED: Whenever a body is overtaxed mentally or physically the Radial Appliance is helpful to produce normal rest. The Appliance is designed to equalize the circulatory vibrations of a body; hence any condition which directly disturbs the circulation is improved through its regular use. It has been used successfully in the treatment of rheumatism, neuralgia, headaches, colds, insomnia, fatigue, and overwrought nerves.

In some instances the Radial Appliance directions call for the use of a solution, such as Gold Chloride, Iodine, Camphor, etc. When this is the case . . . a special attachment can be supplied with the Appliance. This special attachment consists of a small jar holding the solution, through which passes a hollow lead tubing. One wire from the appliance is attached to the solution so that the current from the body passes through it.

DIRECTIONS FOR USING THE RADIAL APPLIANCE: The Appliance should be placed in the crock and surrounded with cracked ice. Add water until it reaches a level of about 2 inches from the top of the Appliance. Do not allow the water to come over the top of the Appliance. Let it stand in this manner for 15 to 20 minutes before attaching to the body, leaving it in the ice water during the time it is attached to the body.

When the Appliance is ready for use, insert the tips of the wires in the holes. DO NOT LET THE METAL DISCS OR PLATES TOUCH EACH OTHER AFTER THE WIRES HAVE BEEN FASTENED TO THE APPLIANCE!

The attachments would be made in this manner:

1st day: The plate coming from the red pole would be attached FIRST, to the RIGHT WRIST; while the other plate coming from the black pole would be attached LAST, to the LEFT ANKLE.

2nd day: FIRST attachment (from the red pole) would be to the LEFT WRIST; LAST attachment (from the black pole) to the RIGHT ANKLE.

3rd day: Attach FIRST to the LEFT ANKLE; LAST to the RIGHT WRIST.

4th day: FIRST to the RIGHT ANKLE; LAST to the LEFT WRIST.

Thus a circle of the body will have been made in the attachments. The first attachment becomes the positive, the last the negative. Thus always be sure to attach FIRST the plate coming from the RED pole, LAST the one coming from the black pole.

Alternate the attachments each day in the manner indicated, for one hour (1 hr.), unless otherwise specified for your particular case. Use for 3 to 4 rounds of the 4-day periods, then leave off a few days, then begin again.

It is preferable to remain quiet, in a prayerful, meditative and constructive attitude during the hour the Appliance is attached, while resting, or just before retiring at night.

Note: The plates are attached to the inside of the wrist, as near the pulse as possible, and to the inside of the ankle–in the hollow just between the ankle joint and the tendon which runs down the back of the leg to the heel. Adjust the bands so that the discs are held securely in place against the skin.

No sensation will be experienced by the body while using

this Appliance, other than possibly a slight tingling in the extremities of the body (hands and feet) or a feeling of drowsiness slowly creeping over the body. Upon awakening the next morning the body will feel thoroughly relaxed and very much refreshed from the night's sleep.

When not using the Appliance, disconnect the wires and if convenient, place the unit in the sun for 20 to 30 minutes. This is all the recharging that will be necessary. Before and after each attachment, be sure the plates are cleaned or polished with the emery cloth which is provided. Special care should be taken not to let them become corroded by the acids and oils from the body.

The vibratory current of the body passes through the Appliance, the temperature of the Appliance being lower than that of the body, building up a low charge, which is given off into the body through the other attachment, completing the circuit. The effect of the Appliance is to equalize the circulation and relieve strain in any congested or taut areas of the nervous system. The action is that of equalizing the natural vibration or current of the body itself.

1800-24 Reports

The Wet Cell Appliance or Wet Cell Battery

The other appliance frequently cited is the Wet Cell. It is recommended in approximately nine hundred readings and was generally suggested for individuals with more severe health problems. Although Cayce indicated that the Wet Cell uses the same vibrational process as the Radial Appliance, the Wet Cell is actually a chemical battery and produces a slight output. It is a chemical battery because the device uses diluted medicinal solutions that the readings state are carried vibrationally into the body to facilitate regeneration and healing. In fact, the readings suggest that medicines taken vibrationally produce fewer side effects.

The Wet Cell is a little more complicated to use. Therefore, anyone interested in pursuing the use of the Wet Cell should explore the directions at the A.R.E. web site: EdgarCayce.org. Oftentimes the solutions recommended to be used with the Wet Cell included gold, which the readings state contain a renewing vibration, or silver, which was cited as possessing a sustaining vibration. (281–27)

From Cayce's perspective, when combined with other treatments, the Wet Cell Battery is often helpful for serious health problems, including cerebral palsy, deafness, paralysis, arteriosclerosis, epilepsy, blindness, tumors, dementia, and various kinds of cancers. One of the instances in which the Wet Cell was recommended was the case of a seventy-year-old man with paralysis resulting from a cerebral hemorrhage. His request for assistance was dated June 1944 and included the following information:

> On August 6, 1942, I suffered a cerebral hemorrhage result-ing hemiplegia left side, rending left arm and leg useless. This condition has existed since, but has responded slightly to treatment which consisted of massage with physical therapy, low wave electric stimulation. The left leg has responded to the extent that I am able to stand on same and walk with assistance for short intervals, but my arm is quite useless. Physical condition at present fairly good. Weight 164, blood pressure ranges 110 to 120 over 70. Pulse 80 to 90. Circulation fair. Temperature normal. Appetite fair. Suffer from extreme nervousness and fear from falling due to dizziness. 5325-1 Background

During the course of the reading, Cayce stated that because of the client's age, his circulation had slowed, causing the "recuperative forces" of his body to slow as well. The reading added that the hemorrhage had caused a lesion, affecting his locomotion. The central recommendation was the Wet Cell Appliance, using a solution containing gold, as the vibration would be helpful. A change of diet containing more vegetables, more easily assimilated foods, and less meats was also recommended, as was massage.

Assuring the client of the efficacy of the appliance, Cayce added, "We may gradually build back better use of both the leg, which is improving, and a better use of the arm, and prevent it from swelling at times." And then, as if responding to any doubt, the reading counseled, "Expect much, you will obtain much! Expect little, you will obtain little! Expect nothing, you will obtain nothing!"

Another case involving the Wet Cell presented itself in the form of a forty-seven-year-old man (a post office foreman, husband, and father of three children) who had been institutionalized after a nervous breakdown and a diagnosis of dementia praecox, a form of mental illness often involving hallucinations. Doctors assumed that the condition had come as a result of stress and overwork. The reading was given while Mr. (1513) was still confined at Rockland State Hospital in New York.

At the beginning of the reading, Cayce stated that the problem was not just a mental condition and that other treatments besides psychological help were required. In fact, the readings suggested that unless those treatments were applied, it was unlikely that Mr. (1513) would be cured and return to his normal life and work. According to the reading, the problem had come as a result of his falling on the ice and injuring his coccyx (an experience that the patient later confirmed). That original injury had led to a circulation problem and then a glandular imbalance that was now affecting his mental health. The essential treatments included a series of osteopathic adjustments to help the spine, and the Wet Cell appliance to address the glandular problem. If the treatments were followed, Cayce promised a "restoring of the mental forces and a better coordination." (1513-1) When it was asked "How long will it be before he will be able to return to work, after leaving the institution?" the reply came, ". . . at least sixty to ninety days."

The treatments were begun and a follow-up reading was obtained a few months later. During the course of that reading, Cayce stated that the coccyx injury had been corrected but that there was still a problem with normalizing the vibrations within the body. It was suggested that this could be corrected by continuing to use the Wet Cell for another six to eight months and working with osteopathic manipulation several times a month. The treatments were followed and by the end of the year, the individual had been healed and had resumed his normal life. In fact, the following report ensued, after Edgar Cayce gave a lecture in December 1938 at the McAlpin Hotel in New York City:

In introducing Mr. Cayce, Mr. David Kahn announced that a

man had just entered the hall whose story he wanted to tell. Mr. Kahn then described this case, [1513]. At the conclusion of the story Mr. [1513] rose from his seat and came to the front of the hall. In a quiet, choked voice he said, "Every word of this is true, and I came tonight to shake the hand of the man who gave me back my life." When Mr. [1513] and Mr. Cayce shook hands, there was hardly a dry eye in the hall.

1/4/39 Letter from [1513] to Edgar Cayce: ". . . Was very pleased to learn that my appearance at your meeting and the short address that I delivered was satisfactory and helpful. Rest assured that I will be at your service whenever you may feel that I have anything in the way of enlightenment to contribute to your audience . . ."   1513-2 Reports

The Wet Cell Appliance was also an integral part of the treatment given to a twenty–something–year–old woman in curing her scleroderma, which is thought to be incurable and results in a gradual hardening of the tissues of the body and eventual death. The young woman, Miss (528), had previously been helped by the readings for a problem with severe acne, so when she was diagnosed with scleroderma, Cayce was contacted for help. In a 1961 interview with Hugh Lynn Cayce, the woman described her experience with the readings:

I became ill about eight months before I obtained the first reading for the condition [528-3] on 1/14/37. I was examined at the Haggert Clinic in Nashville, Tenn. At first I had symptoms something like flu or malaria. That is what they first thought I had. There was a generalized aching all over the body, and a low-grade temperature. By the time I had the reading I was hard–all the flesh from the hips to the knees was just as hard as it could be. I was not suffering pain, except just the aching. All the upper part of my body was swollen, and when I smiled my face was so swollen that I couldn't see out of my eyes. I had a pone [hardness] all down my back, and my arms were swollen. I was swollen all over my body except from my knees to my feet, and from my hips to my thighs the flesh was *hard*. My condition was getting progressively worse at the time I obtained the reading. The main treatment, as I remember, was Castor Oil Packs. I had to lie in these packs for three hours at a time, three times a day; in for three hours and out for two hours, and there was some medication but I have forgotten what it was. A little later the Wet Cell Appliance was recommended, and I did use it. Later on the olive oil rubs were advised.

In a week's time after beginning the treatments the swelling began to leave my face, and it just gradually left. By the summer of 1937 the swelling was just in my thighs a little bit. In September of 1937 I went back to work, as an organist at the Methodist Church.

Yes, I completely recovered. In 1942 I got married and am still married but have no children. I am still active as an organist and have had no return of the trouble.

528-16 Reports

More than fifty years after Miss (528) received her first reading, another woman was diagnosed with scleroderma, by the Layhe clinic in Massachusetts. She started using the Cayce approach to scleroderma in May 1991, working in conjunction with a doctor sympathetic to Cayce's treatment modalities, and made the following report to her doctor in March 1992:

I'm writing you this letter to inform you of the results of my tests I had run at Layhe clinic. I went to Layhe on February 4, 5, 6. They did a pulmonary test which measured the amount of air I take into my lungs and checked my blood gases. I'm pleased to tell you the test turned out great. My lungs have improved from last year. I have 97% oxygen in my blood. The doctors couldn't believe it. They said that they had never seen that before. When you have a thickening of the lung, as I did, it does not improve. It can stay the same, but it will not improve. Well, Doc, we proved them wrong. I'm living proof it can happen. I wish you could have been there to see how confused they were because they couldn't explain it. Was great! . . .
Sincerely, [signed] C.S.

As stated previously, the Wet Cell Battery was included as treatment for a variety of conditions, including toxemia in the case of a twenty-five-year-old man with severe gingivitis. His actual diagnosis had been labeled by a physician as "idiopathic gingivitis, metabolic deficiency and colonic stasis." His teeth and gums were black, and his mouth was so sore that he could not eat. Doctors at Johns-Hopkins hospital stated that he needed silver in his system, but they did not know how to safely administer it. Working with the vibration of silver nitrate proved to be part of the answer. Although for a time he had considered suicide because of the pain he was in, he was eventually healed of his condition and lived until 1979. (1455-3)

The Cayce archives also include the Wet Cell as a portion of the suggested course of treatment in the case of a forty-six-year-old woman afflicted with stomach ulcers. Once again, it was the effect that the appliance had on vibrations that seemed to be a part of the rationale for the treatment. (The woman lived to be in her mid-eighties.) The reading included the following statement:

> **Then, in meeting those conditions in the present, we would find that with the low form of electrical vibration given, so that the effects of same pass directly *through* the system itself, would tend to disintegrate those vibrations that are set up at present as *impulses* from that particular center that has been under strain and stress.** **482-3**

In 1938 Dr. Mary Miller, who had worked with several of the cases in the Cayce files, presented three individuals at a New York program. One of the individuals was a thirty-four-year-old woman who was almost completely blind (1496). Another was a fifty-three-year old woman with breast cancer (1500), and the third was a fifty-year-old woman with severe arthritis (1517). For the cases involving breast cancer and arthritis, Cayce recommended the Wet Cell battery. For the woman with breast cancer, the overall rational for treatment recommended by the readings included "vibratory forces and manipulations" (1500-2). For the woman with arthritis, the treatment included a weak solution of chloride of gold, carried vibrationally by the Wet Cell battery. During the course of the reading, Cayce told the woman, "This is a very weak solution, but if it is carried vibratorially in this manner it will be sufficient in the beginning." (1517-1) All three women had been cured of their conditions by following treatments outlined in the readings.

As discussed with the Radial Appliance, the effectiveness of Cayce's treatments was dependent upon the patient's willingness or ability to carry them out. One example of failure in terms of the Wet Cell was the case of a fifty-nine-year-old man with cancer as well as kidney and liver problems. In addition to dietary recommendations, internal medications, and massage, the reading included the following: "We would begin with the use of the low electrical vibrations as come from the Wet Cell Appliance that would carry into the system the vibrations from the atomic iodine (that is, Atomidine) and the Spirits of Camphor; one given one day, one given the next day." (1209-1)

Immediately after the reading was given, the following report was filed: "Mr. [1209]'s wife says the reading fits his symptoms, but just what action she intends to take she has not said. There are 4-5 doctors on the case, and they seem to think Mr. [1209] will not live much longer." Within a few months, Mr. (1209) had died. A notation was made in the file by Cayce's secretary that she did not think they ever carried out the suggestions in his reading.

Eventually, all individuals who had the Wet Cell battery referenced in their readings received a handout, with directions for using the appliance. An excerpt from that original handout (ca. 1940) is referenced below; as mentioned previously, complete instructions for using the Wet Cell Appliance are available from A.R.E.'s web site: EdgarCayce.org.

WET CELL APPLIANCES

Extract from Reading 1800-4. "The human body is made up of electronic vibrations, with each atom and element of the body, each organ and organism of same, having its electronic unit of vibration necessary for the sustenance of, and equilibrium in, that particular organism. Each unit, then, being a cell or a unit of life in itself, has its capacity of reproducing itself by the first law as is known of repro-duction–division. When a force in any organ, or element of the body, becomes deficient in its ability to reproduce that equilibrium necessary for the sustenance of the physical existence and reproduction of same, that portion becomes deficient through electronic energy as is necessary. This may come by injury or disease, received from external forces. It may come from internal forces through lack of eliminations produced in the system, or by the lack of other agencies to meet the requirements of same in the body."

Even a strain or binding in the body will cause incoordination. Impulses, as messages, will not reach the different parts of the body properly. The circulation will thus be affected and inflammation will result.

The action of the Wet Cell Appliance, described here, deals with a vibratory theory. The nervous systems, the circulation and the ductless glands are the parts of the body particularly involved.

This appliance is used with a solution which in itself generates a low electrical current. The ingredients are Copper Sulphate, Sulphuric Acid, Willow Charcoal, and Zinc. Two poles of nickel and copper extend into the solution contained in a heavy crock. To the ends of the poles wire leads are attached and extend to the body of the individual. Chemical compounds may also be carried through this Appliance.

One of the leads form the Appliance passes through a container holding the desired chemical solution. To the ends of the wire leads various types of metal anodes are attached, according to the chemical being used.

It is interesting to note that the anodes of this Appliance are placed at special nerve centers along the cerebrospinal system and over ducts and glands in the frontal portion of a body. The impulse of the low electrical current is sent direct to the centers needing attention, and works through the nervous systems rather than through the circulatory system. The principle of the influence of the atomic vibrations is the same as with the Radio-Active [Radial] Appliance (another type of appliance which has evolved from the study and the application of Mr. Cayce's Readings.) The difference lies primarily, we believe, in that the Radio-Active [Radial] works through the circulation and the Wet Cell through the nervous systems direct to the ducts and glands affected.

The Wet Cell Appliances have been recommended in serious cases of incoordination with undeveloped children, in paralytic cases, for gland conditions and serious nervous disorders involving insanity. We have in our files reports on cases of arthritis, paralysis, and brain disorders, where definite help has been received. Where this type of treatment is recommended, the case is generally of a very serious nature and requires patience and persistence in carrying out the needed treatments.

Research work on these appliances is still in elementary stages. In keeping with the general policy of the Association, we welcome the cooperation and interest of all members interested in this phase of the work. These appliances (the Radio-Active [Radial] and the Wet Cell) have been developed from detailed descriptions and explanations given through the psychic Readings of Edgar Cayce. They have been used with highly gratifying results by members over a period of many years. The work of presenting these appliances to the scientific world, and to the thousands who may benefit from using them, becomes one of the privileges and duties of those who glimpse a vision of their possible value to humanity.   5341-1 Background

The Violet Ray

During Edgar Cayce's lifetime, various forms of electrotherapy were used by a variety of healthcare professionals for many conditions. The Violet Ray is a high voltage, low amperage source of static electricity, which was in common use during the 1920s and 30s. It was recommended for a variety of purposes, including stimulation of circulation and the nervous systems. The Cayce readings usually prescribed its use in conjunction with other treatments, such as osteopathic adjustments or massage.

For example, the Violet Ray was recommended in the case of a fifty-three-year-old woman with severe arthritis, poor circulation, and problems with her eliminations. Confined to a wheelchair because of her debilitating condition, the readings recommended a thirty-minute massage every other day, from the base of the brain to the spine and then throughout the shoulder blades and arms. Afterward, the Violet Ray was to be used over the same areas. Cayce described the importance of the Violet Ray: ". . . the activities of the violet ray are only to make for the electrical rejuvenation of nerve energies that have been depleted through the inactivity of the whole system of the body." An internal medication was also recommended, as was a complete change of diet:

> **We would be mindful, too, that the diets are rather of the semi-liquid or semi-solid foods, that will not make for too great a heaviness. But let one meal each day, whether morning, noon or night, be of *raw* vegetables–combined in a salad or eaten separately; such as lettuce, celery, carrots, beets, turnips, spinach, peppers, tomatoes, cabbage (white and red)–all of these may be used, or they may be used in pod, but at least some time during each day let all of these in their *various* ways be combined, you see. The other meals should be of those foods such as indicated, and no great heavy amount.   676-1**

If the treatments were followed, Cayce promised, "We will have the body walking!"

On another occasion, a woman had heard about the Edgar Cayce work through a popular article in *Coronet* magazine. Because she was having problems with menopause, doctors eventually performed a hysterectomy. Since the operation, however, the woman had been having severe problems with depression, nervousness, headaches, obesity, and insomnia. Along with the woman's request for help, her husband submitted the following observations: "She has been feeling this way for years. Doctors can't see anything outstanding and won't pay any attention to her. Operation about 3 yrs. ago [hysterectomy], since which she has been perhaps a little worse." (3386-1)

Cayce began the reading by stating, "There are disturbances that become very aggravating to the body at times. We find that these have to do primarily with tie-ups in the nervous systems." He then went on to describe the functioning of the blood supply and circulation, the woman's nerves and her cerebrospinal and sympathetic nervous systems, and the body's organs and digestion. After describing the overall condition of the woman, he went on to provide the recommended course of treatment:

> In making applications for corrective forces, we find that these should be the manners:
>
> First we would begin using the Violet Ray each evening when ready to retire, the bulb applicator partially in the 9th dorsal area and around the body at the diaphragm area, at the areas between the shoulders and up to the head. These treatments should go up and down on either side of the spine, rather than on the spine itself, but cross the areas at the 9th dorsal, the 1st, 2nd, 3rd dorsal, 3rd cervical and 1st and 2nd cervical. Use the bulb applicator for about twenty minutes not longer, and this should be a daily or an evening performance–when ready to retire–applying it directly to the body.
>
> Each week have a thorough relaxing treatment osteopathically. This should never be a stimulating treatment, and should not be done so as to get through with it in two or three minutes; but slowly, easily, relax the body, first in the 1st, 2nd, 3rd, 4th cervical–on either side of same; then the 1st, 2nd 3rd, 4th dorsals–then in the 9th dorsal. These should be released, but relaxed and then the releasing. This should require at least twenty to thirty minutes for a gentle massage to relax the body thoroughly.
>
> Add to the body the vitamins in the order as they may apply to body building forces. These at first will appear to make the body gain more weight; then as corrections osteopathically are made there will be the tendency to correct the body as to weight and as to activity. These vitamins should be in the combination called KalDak. For this body, take this in the V-8 juices; half a teaspoonful once each day, dissolved thoroughly in a very little hot water, then–not a full tumbler but a small glass, as an orange juice glass, filled with the V-8 combination of juices. Drink this

about three or four o'clock in the afternoon, and it will help
to pick the body up. It will give strength and vitality.

Then, sing a lot about the work–in everything the body
does. Hum, sing–to self; not to be heard by others but to be
heard by self.

As to the diet, keep away from fats of most every nature.
This doesn't mean not to eat butter when you can get it, but
don't eat the fats of beef, rarely ever any beef. Fish, fowl and
lamb may be taken, but never fried foods.

Have at least three vegetables above the ground to one
that grows beneath the ground.

Do these and we will bring better conditions for this body.

3386-1

According to the notations on file, the woman did find relief from
her condition. In fact, during a follow–up report in 1952, the individual
had this to say:

Before my first reading I had had an operation called
hysterectomy–the removal of uterus, ovaries and tubes
(Fallopian). After the massage and the violet-ray apparatus
the insomnia was much improved and in a few weeks I was
sleeping like a baby and still am. Singing helps a great deal
to keep myself in a cheerful frame of mind. At the time I was
dreadfully morbid and depressed mentally caused by
menopause, brought on prematurely by the drastic operation at my early age. My husband [5224] died 11/16/47. It is
very lonely without him and I am looking forward to being
with him in the not so far distant future.

Although other electrotherapeutic treatments received mention in
the Cayce readings, the Radial Appliance, the Wet Cell, and the Violet
Ray were the most often recommended appliances for helping the
individual. Somehow these appliances help to generate electrical energy
that is therapeutic in reestablishing the vibrations within the organ or
body itself. As Cayce told one individual, "For, all life is electrical energy."
(3491-1)

The general approach for working with any of the appliances

for healing mentioned in the Edgar Cayce readings was perhaps best expressed to a twenty-nine-year-old woman suffering with scleroderma:

> **Keep the constructive forces in much of the prayer and meditation, and especially in the periods when the Appliance is used. Raise that vibration within self that there *are* within self the healing forces. For all healing of every nature comes only from the One Source, the Giver of all good and perfect gifts.**   **528-10**

Miscellaneous Appliances for Assisting Humankind

As the knowledge of what Edgar Cayce could do spread, and along with it the understanding that he was somehow able to access virtually any information while in the unconscious state, the requests for readings began to expand and explore a variety of fascinating questions. In terms of the subject of vibrations and the appliances, some of the most interesting topics explored by the Cayce readings deal with the Aurascope, the Perpetual Motion Machine, and the Radio Static Eliminator. Each of these is discussed briefly below.

The Aurascope

Although it was only mentioned in four readings, given to the same individual (440-3, 440-6, 440-7, and 440-12), the possibilities presented by what Cayce called the "Aurascope" are quite fascinating. First mentioned in 1933 to a twenty-three-year-old student and electrical engineer, the readings suggested that it would be possible to create a machine that could "see" the aura around individuals. From Cayce's perspective, the aura is a vibrational energy field that emanates from all living things. This aura provides a pictorial representation of an individual's energy, health, state of mind, thoughts, possibilities, and potentials. It also contains information related to a person's talents, weaknesses, karmic lessons, and past lives. The readings suggested that once created, this machine would enable individuals with any degree of psychic ability to perceive someone's aura and diagnose his or her physical, mental, and spiritual well–being.

The readings described the machine and its ability to perceive vibrations and various colors (suggesting the health, well–being, state of mind, etc., of whatever was being perceived):

> **As suggested, the theory of the mechanical device is to determine not only the aura of individuals but to use same in the diagnoses of disorders in various portions of the body.**
>
> **As is known, the body in action–or a live body–emanates from same the vibrations to which it as a body is vibrating, both physical and spiritual. Just as there is an aura when a string of a musical instrument is vibrated–the tone is produced by the vibration. In the body the tone is given off rather in the higher vibration, or the color. Hence this is a condition that exists with each physical body.   440-6**

According to notations on file in the Cayce archives, over the years several individuals followed the instructions provided by the readings for creating an Aurascope. Although several prototypes have been created, no fully working model of this particular appliance has ever been produced.

The Perpetual Motion Machine[5]

Over a period of several years, the readings explored the possibility of perpetual motion in a series of thirty–some readings (see especially, 195-51, 195-52, 195-56, 195-57, 195-59 through 195-67, 195-69, 195-70, 900-464, 3657-1, 3989-1, 4665-2 through 4665-4, 4665-6, 4665-7, 4665-9, 4665-11 through 4665-13). Essentially three individuals (Marion Stansell, Tim Brown, and Morton Blumenthal) utilized the Cayce source as a means for the creation of a motor that was said to possess the capability

---

[5] The story behind the perpetual motion machine (also known as the Stansell motor) is told in greater detail in the chapter "Gravity, Polarity, and Perpetual Motion" of Sidney D. Kirkpatrick's *Edgar Cayce: An American Prophet.*

of revolutionizing technology. On one occasion, when asked to describe how the perpetual motion was generated, Cayce offered the following:

> **Elements of the active principle in that called *now* generated energy, or the breaking of the vibratory unit to begin its expansion in force. As is in gravitation. In gravitation– *commonly* known–is that everything sinks to a common center, or is *drawn* to a common center; while that as is expanded is the positive energy in opposite relation to that force drawing. One goes up, the other we say goes down–as you would commonly express it. This is a very crude way, to say one goes up and one goes down–because it continues a circular motion in its activity, in this force.   195-54**

The readings predicted that the motor, once perfected, would be of such commercial value that it would generate $10 million dollars (in 1929 dollars!) to underwrite and support Atlantic University, which had been founded by Cayce, Blumenthal, and others one year earlier. Although a number of prototypes were created and various readings were given on fixing and perfecting the prototypes as well as patenting the motor, a workable perpetual motion machine was never completed. The machine remains just one of the many untapped potentials contained within the Edgar Cayce readings.

The Static Eliminator

In 1924, prior to the commercial popularity of radio in the 1940s and 1950s, Edgar Cayce was asked to give the directions for creating a device that would help to eliminate radio static. The question resulted in a series of readings (the 2492 series and the 1497) in which the device was described, as was the interconnection between radio wave transmissions and vibrations. During one of those readings, when asked to describe why static occurred, Cayce offered the following:

> **We know that all force is created by vibration. We know that all vibration becomes electrical in its action and its effect. That is, it either enlivens, bring greater vibration, or being**

under vibration becomes deadened or destructive to one or the other of the vibrations thus met.

That law governing then the vibrations in transmission of messages, as is called radio, is the relativity of vibration as set in motion in any one particular place, and other vibrations attuned to that same vibration receiving through the electrical waves, created by the one through the receiving forces, magnified in the other . . .

We have given as here as how the vibration, as now called static, may be eliminated, which is, in other words, giving the tone to the vibration as created by the sending ring when received in the receiving set as now in force. That is, the vibration in rings, in circles, as is set, raised by electrical forces, until we produce the equal magnified forces to receive and make them understandable in the receiving sets . . .

All force (for the law again) we find is ever present in every atom of vibration, and is subject to all laws of heat and cold and of the other vibrations in the air, or in the vacuum created from time to time by changes, this creating more effect on the vibratory force than other vibrations, for each are in themselves. With the colors we eliminate, for in these we will create the rest.   2492-5

In spite of the fact that the device was explored in more than twenty readings, a commercially viable prototype was never created. However, the readings suggested that the static eliminator would eventually be of much worth to humanity. Perhaps at some point in the future, someone will find value in understanding the activities of vibrations through the atmosphere and discover a potential for this device in the age of wireless Internet–and–cell–phone proliferation.

VIBRATIONS
Miscellaneous Vibrations

For each and every atomic force throws off a vibration to which a sensitive soul becomes aware.   *1189-1*

FROM THE PERSPECTIVE OF THE **E**DGAR **C**AYCE READINGS, everything is an aspect of the one force and vibration. In addition to vibrations as they relate to healing, locations, sound, color, and materiality, Cayce discussed various aspects of vibrations in terms of the vibrations of names, numbers, consciousness, and even the "generative force," which somehow impelled action into various directions. For example, when an eighteen-year-old student received a Life reading in 1942, exploring his talents and abilities and the suggested direction for his life's work, Edgar Cayce stated that he would excel in any career that dealt with the "fields of vibration." According to the readings, this kind of work would enable him to manifest his soul talents and cultivate his relationship with the divine. The readings' advice included the following:

As to the abilities of the entity in the present–these are limitless, if that which is the power of Creative Forces is taken as the director, the partner in same.

In the fields of vibration, in the fields of vibration as related to economic conditions, as well as in the generating forces in growth of mineral, vegetable and animal kingdoms, the entity may–with application–find the outlets for self's abilities; though keep thy head high, thy feet grounded in the faith in Him. 2850-1

Another interesting concept related to vibrations that comes out of the Edgar Cayce information is the fact that names are empowered with a vibrational quality that impels individuals in certain directions or somehow enables them to more readily manifest specific qualities or attributes. In fact, the readings suggest that the soul often has an impact upon the consciousness of the parents as they are in the process of naming their offspring. In addition to that, the readings contend that an individual's name may carry some similarity from one incarnation to the next, as the name often embodies the overall vibration and consciousness of the individual. On one occasion, this notion that individuals are not named by chance was explained to the Glad Helpers Prayer Group:

Hence the name is relative to that which *is* accomplished by the soul *in* its sojourn throughout its whole experience; whether in those environs about this individual sphere or another . . .

Was one named John by chance? Was one named Joe or Llewellyn by chance? No; they are relative! While it may be truly in the material plane relative because you have a rich aunt by that name, or relative because an uncle might be named that–but these carry then the vibrations of same; and in the end the name is the sum total of what the soul-entity in all of its vibratory forces has borne toward the Creative Force itself.

Hence each soul has a definite influence upon the experiences through which it may be passing. 281-30

While exploring the interpretation of the Revelation, the prayer group received additional information on this interconnection between vibrations and names. This information contends that ultimately, each individual is known by a unique soul name to somehow designate that soul from all others:

> **Each entity, each soul, is known—in all the experiences through its activities—as a name to designate it from another. It is not only then a material convenience, but it implies—as has been given, unless it is for material gain—a definite period in the evolution of the experience of the entity in the material plane . . .**
>
> **For what meaneth a name? John, Jane, Peter, Andrew, Bartholomew, Thaddeus, Rhoda, Hannah? All of these have not only the attunement of vibration but of color, harmony; and all those relative relationships as one to another.   281-31**

Because of the importance of a name and its vibrations, on a number of occasions the readings would actually suggest a specific name or a nickname for an individual, as is evidenced in the following case histories.

Edgar Cayce told the parents of a newborn baby girl that their daughter should be named "Elizabeth Carol." (2391-1) Apparently, the vibration best suited the abilities that the soul hoped to manifest in the present as well as the fact that the soul had also been named Elizabeth in her most recent incarnation.

On another occasion, parents of a two-day-old girl were told to name their child "Lilith Ann," as it would assist her in manifesting the personality and talents and abilities she required in the present. (1958-1) Actually, the readings suggested specific names for newborn infants on a number of occasions. According to notations in the Cayce archives, the advice was generally followed (for example 299-1, 1208-1, 1346-1, 2824-1, and others).

During the course of a Life reading given to the parents of an eight-year-old boy who was often referred to by the nickname "Sonny," the readings advised that his nickname should be changed to "Bart." The rationale was in part due to the fact that the soul had been named Barton Sawswythe during an incarnation around the time of the American Revolution, and the soul was apparently attempting to manifest many of the same talents and abilities in the present. (305-3)

Similarly, when a twenty-six-year-old businessman with the first name Edwin and the middle name David asked why his readings generally referred to him by his middle name, the readings provided the following:

> The development of the entity is rather in that vibration of David than of Edwin for these two conditions are with the vibration in names: Eddie, Edwin (first name), meaning that of a peacefulness, defender of peacefulness, carrying both the condition and implied forces from same. David, rather that of the gift from the higher forces, or a son of the Father. One, especially, endowed with gifts from the higher forces.
> **137-13**

During one reading given to a twenty-one-year-old harpist, Cayce suggested that her name, Margaret, carried the perfect vibration for which she had entered into the earth, which was essentially the desire to be used as a healing channel by the Creative Forces through her music—a gift that often inspired others to find their own relationship to the divine. In the language of the readings,

> In the development then of the soul forces of this entity, Margaret, called in the present, as has been given, the title, the name, is written; that is, there is the desire, there is the wish, there is the longing to be used by self, to use self, to be used by the Creative Forces in giving to others that which will in themselves arouse the understanding and the knowledge of the indwelling of the spiritual life within self that may quicken the soul to its own duties, opportunities, abilities, as related to *their* influences and *their* relationships with the Creative Forces. Hence is the title, is the name written within self, and recorded with those that have given His angels charge concerning thine activities, that there be

no stumbling within the experience of this soul.   275-39

It was because of the different vibrations carried by each name that a woman who used the nickname "Tillie" was advised instead to use her real name, Burlynn. The readings explained the different vibrational qualities of each name in response to the thirty-year-old woman's questions: "What vibrations do the names Burlynn and Tillie carry? Please explain the different response to each name. Should Burlynn continue to cultivate her nickname of 'Tillie', or eliminate one or the other?"

> **Names have their vibration. To be sure, names have their element of influence or force, by the very activity of the name.**
>
> **Burlynn indicates *strength*, virility; and Tillie almost the opposite! [Years later, the woman reported: "I can see the point. Calling me Tillie always made me feel sort of cocky, and I'm not the cocky type."]   934-7**

Just as each individual possesses a name and that name corresponds to a certain level of vibration, from Cayce's perspective, each individual also possesses a number, or rather, vibrates to the energy of a specific number. When a forty-seven-year-old investment banker asked for additional information on numerology during the course of his Life reading and whether or not numerology could be used to enhance his psychic ability, Cayce explained the energetic component of numerology:

> **As we have indicated oft, astrology and numerology and symbology are all but the gateways or the signs of expression.**
>
> **As for this entity, as we have indicated the symbols of numerology may be developed; but the *intuitive* forces that arise *with* same make for rather the safer, the saner, the more spiritual way, with the less aptitude of turning to forces from without.**
>
> **For, as we see in numbers, or numerology: One indicates**

strength, power, influence; yet has all the weaknesses of all other influences that may be brought to bear upon any given activity in which same may be indicated. But it is *known* as strength and power; even as the *union* of self with the Creative Forces that express themselves in the activity of matter, in *any* form, is power.

Two makes for a division; yet in the multiple of same, in four, it makes for the greater weaknesses in the divisions. In six and eight it makes for the same characterizations, yet *termed* more in these that one is power, two is weakness, three is the strength of one with the weakness of two; four being more and more of a division and weakness; six being the changes that have been made in the *double* strength of three. Seven is the spiritual number. Eight indicates the commercial change. Nine indicates strength and power, with a change.

These, then, are as *indications*; and *not* other than the *signs* of things, that may be altered ever by the force or factor from which they emanate.   261-15

The vibrational quality of numbers was also explored, during the course of a reading requested by Edgar Cayce himself, as the basis for a talk on numerology that he planned to give:

Then, what form, what force, has given the most perfect illustration of *how* numbers–either in individual life or individuals' experiences in life–affect individuals; or the numbers themselves, and as individuals, or 1, 2, 3, 4, 5, 6, [7], 8, 9, 10, 11, 12, *or* what not–how do the *numbers themselves* value? Possibly the best authority on such is that of the Talismanic, or that obtained from the Talmud–which is a combination of the ancient Persian or Chaldean, Egyptian, Indian, Indo-China, and such.

One is the beginning, to be sure. Before *one* is nothing. After *one* is nothing, if all be *in one*–as *one* God, *one* Son, *one* Spirit. This, then, the *essence* of *all* force, *all* manners of energies. All activities *emanate* from the *one*.

Two–the *combination*, and begins a division of the whole, or the One. While *two* makes for strength, it *also* makes for weakness. This is *illustrated* in that of your music, of your paintings, of your metals, of *whatever* element we may consider!

Three–again a combination of One and Two; this making for strength, making for–in division–that ability of Two *against* One, or One against Two. In *this* strength is seen, as in the Godhead, and is as a greater strength in the whole of combinations.

Again, in *four*, we find that of a division–and while a beauty in strength, in the divisions also makes for the greater weakness–as may be illustrated as in the combinations seen in metal, or numbers, or music, or color.

Five–as seen, a change–as may be seen in a comparison of any of the forces outlined.

Six–again makes for the *beauty* and the symmetrical forces of *all numbers*, making for strength;

As does *seven* signify the *spiritual* forces, as are seen in all the ritualistic orders of any nature; as seen in the dividing up of conditions, whether they be of the forces in nature or those that react to the sensual forces of man in any character.

Eight–again showing that combination in strength, also a combination in weakness;

Nine making for the *completeness* in numbers; yet showing not the strength as of Ten, nor yet the weakness as of Eight, yet making for that termination in the *forces* in natural *order* of things that come as a change imminent in the life.

In *ten* we have those of the completeness as of numbers, and a strength as is found in *few*; yet these are as a combination in the forces as are manifest.

In *eleven* is again seen those of the *beauty* of numbers, yet that weakness as was signified by those of the betrayal in the numbers.

Twelve as a *finished* product, as is given in all forces in nature; as was given in all forces as combined to those of the ritualistic forms, those of the mystic forces, those of the numbers as related to those of a combination; for as of the voices of *twelve* requiring Twenty to even drown same, or to overcome same. The same as may be seen in all of the forces

in nature. *Twelve* **combined forces brought those strengths into the world as of [were] necessary for a replenishing of same.** **5751-1**

A number of readings explained the vibrational quality of numbers and how those numbers related to the specific individual. For example, during the course of a Life reading given to an eighteen–year–old male, Cayce stated that an undergirding principle in the youth's makeup was a desire to finish and complete projects or activities; therefore, the number 9 was of the greatest influence. (1035-1) A forty–six–year–old government auditor was encouraged to pursue the study of numerology—a study that would help him understand, according to Cayce, why his soul had chosen to be born on the twentieth of September during his three most recent incarnations. Twenty was apparently an important vibrational number at the soul level. (3178-1) On another occasion, a fifty–seven–year–old man was told that he vibrated to the energy of an 8:

As to numbers, the two hundred and ninety-sixth day of the year–this brings eight as a *vibration* **for the entity that means an awakening within the inner self to the new possibilities, the new opportunities within self that may make for not only carrying with it the** *abilities* **but the obligations of same as well. For to whom much is given in any manifested form, of him much is required. For** *these* **as we find, my son, are as the basic, elemental principles of truth itself. It is a growing thing, even as the knowledge of God, even as the knowledge of truth, even as the knowledge of life; which all are words, yet mean the variations of expressions of that** *ye,* **my son, would worship as a living God.** **707-1**

In spite of the fact that individuals may often resonate or vibrate to a specific numerological value, apparently, that number can change or be influenced by the activities of each individual. When a thirty–eight–year–old male asked for information on his "soul number," the reading had this to say:

You set that yourself. There's one, two, three, four, five, six, seven, eight, nine–which do you choose? Each has its own vibration. Each individual attunes self. Some days you're a five, some days you're a four, other days you're maybe a one or an eleven!   1861-18

The same individual inquired about increasing the humidity in his apartment during the heating season and was told, "You can increase the humidity within self by the raising of the vibrations within self, so that the cold or the heat may be created within self."

In addition to names and numbers, the readings suggest that vibrations also have an interrelationship with levels of consciousness. Some individuals were even told that they were able to perceive what level of vibration others were corresponding to at any given time, as in the case of a forty-seven-year-old English teacher who possessed the ability to tune in to the vibrations of people, situations, and places. (3345-1) A ten-year-old girl, receiving a reading on allergies, was told that she was also affected by the "radiations," or vibrations, of the things that she was allergic to. She asked, "Does coming in contact with flowers, feathers or furs have any effect on this body?" Cayce offered the following: "It does! for there are the radiations from every form of life, and as the plasms as have to do with coagulation are positive, and these of flowers or of any of the pollens that come from same, or vibrations, are negative–then they produce irritation." (2884-1)

On a number of occasions, the readings recommended 2:00 a.m. as an ideal time for meditation because of the higher vibrations at that period of the night–obviously connected, in part, to the inactivity of most individuals and no negative vibrations being created at that time. Similar information was given to a forty-three-year-old woman, who seemed to get a lot of work done in the evening, when she asked, "Do I really get superior vibrations at night enough to justify my working at night rather than day?" Cayce responded, "As we have indicated heretofore, there are those individuals that will find that between one and two or two and two-thirty are the greater periods for work. The vibrations for most are higher during such periods." (846-1)

Another unique concept contained in the Cayce files that is connected to vibrations is the idea of planetary sojourns in consciousness and how these sojourns (and the planets themselves) affect individuals in the present. In brief, the idea is simply that each of the planets represents the vibration of specific lessons in soul growth. After each incarnation, the soul takes stock of its own strengths and weaknesses and may choose to undertake a rigorous lesson in consciousness development that will benefit the soul in future earthly incarnations. For example, a soul needing to know more about love may choose to undertake a period when it is surrounded by the consciousness or vibration of love. That specific energetic vibration corresponds, according to the readings, with the planet Venus. It is important to point out, however, that the soul does not "go" to Venus. Instead, the planet Venus represents the consciousness of love that corresponds to a "sojourn in consciousness" which a specific individual may wish to undertake. On one occasion, Cayce stated, "Each planetary influence vibrates at a different rate of vibration." (281-55)

The readings, at various times, offered the following connections between vibrations and planetary sojourns in consciousness: Uranus is connected to extremes and the psychic. Venus is associated with love. Jupiter is symbolic of the universality of activity or strength. Mercury is related to the mind. Mars is associated with anger or madness. Saturn is connected to trials and woes. Neptune is symbolic of mystical forces, and so forth. (5755-1, 900-10, and others)

And finally, in terms of consciousness and vibrations, the readings assert that communication is possible between the living and the deceased. Most often that communication occurs in the dream state as deceased loved ones attempt to communicate with those they have left behind. However, a series of readings (the "5756 series") was obtained about the possibility of communicating with the spirit plane. That series emphasizes how vibrations play a role in making this type of communication possible. Excerpts from this material follow:

(Q) **Is it possible for those that have passed into the spirit plane to at all times communicate with those in the earth plane?**

(A) **Yes and no—for these conditions are as has been**

described–that the *necessary* way or mode must be prepared; for as this: Ever has that vibration as is attracted and thrown off been active in the world as is exercised through that called the telephone, but without proper connection, without shorts, without any disturbance, may proper communication be made! These have not always been active to the *physical* body. These are not always in proper accord to be used by the physical body. Just the same in that pattern. Those in the astral plane are not always ready. Those in the physical plane are not always ready. What conditions arise (is asked) that we in the physical plane are not ready? The *mind!* . . .

(Q) Is the effort for spirit communication as much effort on the part of the spirit entity as the effort that should be made on the part of the material or physical entity?

(A) The force should never be applied, and may never be applied and be real, in either case. The willingness and the desire from both is necessary for the perfect communication, see? Illustrate this same condition by that physical condition as is seen in attunement of either that called radio, or of that called phone, or that of any of that vibratory force as is set by the electron in the material plane. Necessary for the perfect union that each be in accord. In other words, we find many in the astral plane *seeking* to give force active in the material. Many in the material *seeking* to delve into the astral. They must be made one, would they bring the better.

(Q) What form of consciousness does the spirit entity assume?

(A) That of the subconscious consciousness, as known in the material plane, or the acts and deeds, and thoughts, done in the body, are ever present before that being. Then consider what a hell digged by some, and what a haven and heaven builded by many.   5756-4

Following a personal experience when Edgar Cayce apparently tuned into the communication from deceased loved ones, the readings offered the following explanation:

In giving that which may be helpful, for the moment turn to that known by the body of self and by those present in the room respecting what is ordinarily termed spirit communication–should be (and that which has caused much of the dissension)–*soul* communication. For the soul lives on; and as conditions are only the release of the soul body from a house of clay the activities in the world of matter are only changed in their *relationships* to that which produces same and that the physical body sees in material or three-dimensional form . . .

Here we find, in the experience, that there were those that were in attune–through the vibrations from that sounded in the room at that particular period–and these sought, many–even many that spoke not, to communicate of themselves that there might be known not only their continued existence in a world of matter but of finer matter.

5756-14

From the readings' perspective, all of activity—in fact, all of consciousness—is made possible through the movement of vibrations. Those vibrations have an impact upon all of perception. They energetically empower every thought and every sound. They are integrally woven with motive and with levels of consciousness. They have an ongoing effect upon all of creation.

Conclusion

EVERYTHING IS A MANIFESTATION of the one force moving at different rates of vibration. Vibrations are much more than the ripples of waves atop the water's surface that occur when a stone is dropped from above. Vibrations are a part of the water, of the wave, of the stone, of the air through which the stone descends, of the hand that threw the stone, and even of the thought that led to picking up the stone in the first place. Vibrations are a part of all that exists and all that can be conceived. Everything that exists is vibration.

In more than twenty-five hundred psychic dissertations, Edgar Cayce explored vibrations as really the building blocks of all creation. Vibration is the activity that moves everything into manifestation. Actually, everything is a part of the *one force* manifesting at different levels of vibration. This one force has an ongoing involvement in all aspects of the material world—consciousness, healing, perception, sound—all of physical reality. That force continues to affect each and every one of us.

Since everything is vibration, from this perspective it would be possible to acknowledge that the Creator has also an interrelationship with vibration. Stated another way, even the Creator is an aspect of vibration. With this in mind, the readings would suggest that God continues to interact with each and every soul, every moment of every day, through the manifestation of vibrations—that creative force that empowers all movement, all energy, all life. As Cayce once told a thirty-four-year-old physicist,

> **For, as has been in the experience, and as is partially understood by the entity, everything in motion, everything that has taken on materiality as to become expressive in any kingdom in the material world, is *by* the *vibrations* that are the motions—or those positive and negative influences that make for that differentiation that man has called matter in its various stages of evolution into material things. 699-1**

In addition to their connection with creation and materiality, vibrations are also integrally connected to the evolution of consciousness. From the perspective of the Edgar Cayce readings, one primary purpose of life is to evolve in consciousness in order to be more in attunement with the vibration of the one force that moved all of creation into being in the first place. In 1943 Cayce described the activity of creation by the divine as essentially a movement of vibration:

> **God moved, the spirit came into activity. In the moving it brought light, and then chaos. In this light came creation of that which in the earth came to be matter . . .**
> **Then came into the earth materiality, through the spirit pushing itself into matter. Spirit was individualized, and then became what we recognize in one another as individual entities. Spirit that uses matter, that uses every influence in the earth's environ for the glory of the Creative Forces, partakes of and is a part of the universal consciousness.**
> **3508-1**

On another occasion, the readings stated, ". . . for matter is an expression of spirit in motion [because] . . . In the beginning God created the heavens and the earth. How? The *mind* of God *moved*, and matter, form, came into being." (262–78)

On multiple occasions, the Edgar Cayce information explored the connection between creation and the evolution of vibration, including readings given to the first study group as well as a series of readings given to the Glad Helpers Prayer Group on the Book of Revelation. The idea was also encapsulated in a reading given to a thirty–three–year–old businessman who asked a question regarding the connections between vibration and consciousness. The answer came,

> **As has been given, true it was said, "Come let us make man in our image," in his own image created God, or created by God, was man. Then containing all of the vibrations that were without, were given into that whole being of man— which in *its* vibration gave man the soul. *Above* all else created, see? Then we see how the evolution of force in vibration brought up to the point wherein man becomes one *with* the Creative Energy, or the Godhead . . . 900-422**

At any moment in time, the ongoing development of all creation is discernable through the level of its corresponding vibrations. Contained within the only book he ever wrote personally, *Auras*, Edgar Cayce described this dynamic while discussing the vibrational qualities of the human aura:

> **Every atom, every molecule, every group of atoms and molecules, however simple or complex, however large or small, tells the story of itself, its pattern, its purpose, through the vibrations which emanate from it . . . Thus at any time, in any world, a soul will give off through vibrations the story of itself and the condition in which it now exists.**
> **Cayce, pg. 15**

As the readings themselves state, "Each soul, each entity, has within its inner being the sum of what it has done, is doing, about its relationships to the whole." (2163–1) On one occasion, Cayce scholar Everett Irion took this idea a step further by asserting, "Thus the entire material universe is vibrations moving according to the idea of manifesting their purposes!" (Irion, pg. 34)

All of us are constantly experiencing the impact of the level of vibrations we have helped create and draw toward us. These vibrations are interwoven with the levels of consciousness development that are a portion of the soul's curriculum. Ultimately, however, regardless of how things may appear to the human eye, everything is a part of God. Everything is a part of that one God force in motion. The vibratory levels we may perceive about us and even the infinite ways in which creation appears to manifest are all aspects of the Oneness that is the only true reality. In other words, everything is part of the Oneness of God, and ultimately, the differences we perceive are simply an illusion about that ultimate Oneness:

> **And while secularly or materially these may seem far afield, yet even unto the ends of the earth, even unto the beginning and end of time, the vibration, the truth of those forces of the creative energy are one, and–attuned–these bring those of the same attunement, for *all* are of *one spirit*, and the various variations are those creations as sparks are of that which set same in motion, for all are a portion of that first Creative Energy–God.** 2842-2

Regardless of its form, everything in creation is a part of God. Everything in creation is vibration.

REFERENCES AND RECOMMENDED READING

A.R.E. Meditation Course. Virginia Beach, Virginia: A.R.E. Press. 1978.

A Search for God, Books I & II. 50th Anniversary Edition. Virginia Beach, Virginia: A.R.E. Press. 1992.

Bishop, R.E.D. *Vibration.* London: Cambridge University Press. 1965.

Cayce, Edgar. *Auras.* Virginia Beach, Virginia: A.R.E. Press. 1973.

Emoto, Masaru. *The Hidden Messages in Water.* New York: Atria Books. 2004.

The Holy Bible, King James Version. 1979.

Irion, J. Everett. *Vibrations.* Virginia Beach, Virginia: A.R.E. Press. 1979.

The Jewish Encyclopedia: A Descriptive Record of the History, Religion, Literature, and Customs of the Jewish People from the Earliest Times to the Present Day. London: Funk and Wagnalls Co. 1901.

Jowett, B. *The Works of Plato.* New York: Tudor Publishing Company. N.D.

Kirkpatrick, Sidney D. *Edgar Cayce-An American Prophet.* New York: Riverhead Books: 2000.

McArthur, Bruce. *Your Life: Why It Is the Way It Is and What You Can Do About It.* Virginia Beach, Virginia: A.R.E. Press. 1993.

McMillin, David. "Are We in the Midst of a Renaissance of Atlantean Science and Technology?" *Venture Inward* magazine. Virginia Beach, VA: Association for Research and Enlightenment, Inc. January/February 2007.

Puryear, Herbert Bruce, Ph.D. *Why Jesus Taught Reincarnation: A Better News Gospel.* Scottsdale, Arizona: New Paradigm Press. 1992.

Sugrue, Thomas. *There is a River.* Virginia Beach, Virginia: A.R.E. Press. 1997.

Todeschi, Kevin J. *Edgar Cayce on the Akashic Records.* Virginia Beach, Virginia: A.R.E. Press. 1998.

——. *Edgar Cayce's Twelve Lessons in Personal Spirituality.* Virginia Beach, Virginia: A.R.E. Press. 2005.

——. *Soul Signs: Life Seals, Aura Charts, and the Revelation.* Virginia Beach, Virginia: A.R.E. Press. 2003.

A.R.E. PRESS

Edgar Cayce (1877–1945) founded the non-profit Association for Research and Enlightenment (A.R.E.) in 1931, to explore spirituality, holistic health, intuition, dream interpretation, psychic development, reincarnation, and ancient mysteries—all subjects that frequently came up in the more than 14,000 documented psychic readings given by Cayce.

Edgar Cayce's A.R.E. provides individuals from all walks of life and a variety of religious backgrounds with tools for personal transformation and healing at all levels—body, mind, and spirit.

A.R.E. Press has been publishing since 1931 as well, with the mission of furthering the work of A.R.E. by publishing books, DVDs, and CDs to support the organization's goal of helping people to change their lives for the better physically, mentally, and spiritually.

In 2009, A.R.E. Press launched its second imprint, 4th Dimension Press. While A.R.E. Press features topics directly related to the work of Edgar Cayce and often includes excerpts from the Cayce readings, 4th Dimension Press allows us to take our publishing efforts further with like-minded and expansive explorations into the mysteries and spirituality of our existence without direct reference to Cayce specific content.

A.R.E. Press/4th Dimension Press
215 67th Street
Virginia Beach, VA 23451

Learn more at EdgarCayce.org. Visit ARECatalog.com to browse and purchase additional titles.

ARE PRESS.COM

BAAR PRODUCTS

A.R.E.'s Official Worldwide Exclusive Supplier of Edgar Cayce Health Care Products

Baar Products, Inc., is the official worldwide exclusive supplier of Edgar Cayce health care products. Baar offers a collection of natural products and remedies drawn from the work of Edgar Cayce, considered by many to be the father of modern holistic medicine.

For a complete listing of Cayce-related products, call:

800-269-2502

Or write:

Baar Products, Inc.
P.O. Box 60
Downingtown, PA 19335 U.S.A.
Customer Service and International: 610-873-4591
Fax: 610-873-7945
Web Site: www.baar.com   E-mail: cayce@baar.com

Who Was Edgar Cayce?
Twentieth Century Psychic and Medical Clairvoyant

Edgar Cayce (pronounced Kay-Cee, 1877-1945) has been called the "sleeping prophet," the "father of holistic medicine," and the most-documented psychic of the 20th century. For more than 40 years of his adult life, Cayce gave psychic "readings" to thousands of seekers while in an unconscious state, diagnosing illnesses and revealing lives lived in the past and prophecies yet to come. But who, exactly, was Edgar Cayce?

Cayce was born on a farm in Hopkinsville, Kentucky, in 1877, and his psychic abilities began to appear as early as his childhood. He was able to see and talk to his late grandfather's spirit, and often played with "imaginary friends" whom he said were spirits on the other side. He also displayed an uncanny ability to memorize the pages of a book simply by sleeping on it. These gifts labeled the young Cayce as strange, but all Cayce really wanted was to help others, especially children.

Later in life, Cayce would find that he had the ability to put himself into a sleep-like state by lying down on a couch, closing his eyes, and folding his hands over his stomach. In this state of relaxation and meditation, he was able to place his mind in contact with all time and space—the universal consciousness, also known as the super-conscious mind. From there, he could respond to questions as broad as, "What are the secrets of the universe?" and "What is my purpose in life?" to as specific as, "What can I do to help my arthritis?" and "How were the pyramids of Egypt built?" His responses to these questions came to be called "readings," and their insights offer practical help and advice to individuals even today.

The majority of Edgar Cayce's readings deal with holistic health and the treatment of illness. Yet, although best known for this material, the sleeping Cayce did not seem to be limited to concerns about the physical body. In fact, in their entirety, the readings discuss an astonishing 10,000 different topics. This vast array of subject matter can be narrowed down into a smaller group of topics that, when compiled together, deal with the following five categories: (1) Health-Related Information; (2) Philosophy and Reincarnation; (3) Dreams and Dream Interpretation; (4) ESP and Psychic Phenomena; and (5) Spiritual Growth, Meditation, and Prayer.

Learn more at EdgarCayce.org.

What Is A.R.E.?

Edgar Cayce founded the non-profit Association for Research and Enlightenment (A.R.E.) in 1931, to explore spirituality, holistic health, intuition, dream interpretation, psychic development, reincarnation, and ancient mysteries—all subjects that frequently came up in the more than 14,000 documented psychic readings given by Cayce.

The Mission of the A.R.E. is to help people transform their lives for the better, through research, education, and application of core concepts found in the Edgar Cayce readings and kindred materials that seek to manifest the love of God and all people and promote the purposefulness of life, the oneness of God, the spiritual nature of humankind, and the connection of body, mind, and spirit.

With an international headquarters in Virginia Beach, Va., a regional headquarters in Houston, regional representatives throughout the U.S., Edgar Cayce Centers in more than thirty countries, and individual members in more than seventy countries, the A.R.E. community is a global network of individuals.

A.R.E. conferences, international tours, camps for children and adults, regional activities, and study groups allow like-minded people to gather for educational and fellowship opportunities worldwide.

A.R.E. offers membership benefits and services that include a quarterly body-mind-spirit member magazine, *Venture Inward*, a member newsletter covering the major topics of the readings, and access to the entire set of readings in an exclusive online database.

Learn more at EdgarCayce.org.

EDGARCAYCE.ORG